Business Gamification

FOR

DUMMIES®

Jon,
Welcome to the
team! Badgeville FTW!

Kris

Business Gamification FOR DUMMIES®

by Kris Duggan, CEO of Badgeville,
and Kate Shoup

WILEY

John Wiley & Sons, Inc.

Business Gamification For Dummies®

Published by
John Wiley & Sons, Inc.
111 River St.
Hoboken, NJ 07030-5774
www.wiley.com

Copyright © 2013 by John Wiley & Sons, Inc., Hoboken, New Jersey

Published by John Wiley & Sons, Inc., Hoboken, New Jersey

Published simultaneously in Canada

For general information on our other products and services, please contact our Customer Care Department within the U.S. at 877-762-2974, outside the U.S. at 317-572-3993, or fax 317-572-4002.

For technical support, please visit www.wiley.com/techsupport.

Wiley publishes in a variety of print and electronic formats and by print-on-demand. Some material included with standard print versions of this book may not be included in e-books or in print-on-demand. If this book refers to media such as a CD or DVD that is not included in the version you purchased, you may download this material at http://booksupport.wiley.com. For more information about Wiley products, visit www.wiley.com.

Library of Congress Control Number: 2012955834

ISBN 978-1-118-46693-3 (pbk); ISBN 978-1-118-46694-0 (ebk); ISBN 978-1-118-46695-7 (ebk); ISBN 978-1-118-46696-4 (ebk)

Manufactured in the United States of America

10 9 8 7 6 5 4 3 2 1

WILEY

About the Authors

Kris Duggan, CEO of Badgeville, Inc., is a serial entrepreneur with a passion for building innovative, fast-growing companies. He is dedicated to helping new brands increase user engagement through social gaming and loyalty. A sought-after speaker on gamification, analytics, and user engagement, Kris is a thought leader who specializes in innovative ways to incorporate game mechanics and social loyalty programs into web and mobile experiences. Prior to founding Badgeville, Duggan worked in leadership roles at a variety of successful companies, including WebEx, and across a wide variety of verticals. He lives in Palo Alto with his wife Leah and two sons, Colin and Aidan.

Kate Shoup, during the course of her career, has authored more than 25 books, including *Starting an Etsy Business For Dummies*, *What Can You Do with a Major in Business?*, *Rubbish: Reuse Your Refuse*, *Webster's New World English Grammar Handbook*, and *Office 2010 Simplified* (all published by John Wiley & Sons, Inc.), and has edited scores more. Kate also co-wrote a feature-length screenplay (and starred in the ensuing film) and worked as the sports editor for *NUVO* newsweekly. When not writing, Kate, an IndyCar fanatic, loves to ski (she was once nationally ranked), read, craft, and ride her motorcycle. She also plays a mean game of 9-ball. Kate lives in Indianapolis with her lovely boyfriend, her brilliant daughter, and their dog.

Dedication

For Colin and Aidan.

— Kris Duggan

For Heidi-bird, as always.

— Kate Shoup

Authors' Acknowledgments

I would like to thank Maynard Webb, an early investor in Badgeville, a tech visionary, and an overall inspiring human being. You saw the opportunity for the gamification market before anyone else did. You've been an incredible mentor and advocate for me personally. I'm proud to be associated with your legacy. Many thanks goes to Kate Shoup, who was able to organize and herd the brilliant freneticism that is the Badgeville team and turn it into accessible, palatable content for readers. And Tim Chang, who's earned the right to be called the "Godfather" of gamification — you're always a step ahead of where the market is and have always shaped my views on the "where is this all going?" question. In addition to believing in Badgeville and investing in our success, you are an amazing speaker and advocate for gamification. I'm proud to consider you a friend and a business ally. Thanks to my parents — you guys both believed in me from the beginning. Dad's been an entrepreneur for a long time. And Mom, I'm sure you would have backed anything that your son was going to do, but I feel fortunate that the idea I had (and you believed in) turned out to be a good one! And thanks to Leah, Colin, and Aidan: Many sacrifices are required to get a new company off the ground, particularly one that's grown as fast as Badgeville in the last two and a half years. It's meant a lot of early mornings and late nights, not to mention all the travel. Amidst all the success, I've cherished making it home for dinner as many nights as I can, and catching the kids' baseball games.

— Kris Duggan

Although much of any writer's day is spent alone, desperately pulling words from the ether, no book could be completed without a team of very smart people — and this book is no exception. Indeed, I have many people to thank for their considerable efforts.

First, thanks to Kris Duggan, gamification expert extraordinaire. I simply would not have been given the opportunity to write this book were it not for Kris. In addition to Kris, several other Badgeville folks were extraordinarily helpful with this project. They include Chris Lynch, who, in addition to fielding countless questions throughout the writing process, possesses exceptional beer pong skills; Sam Chou and Joseph Dang, who prevented my suicide by agreeing to help me run down permissions for the various images used in this book; Lily Alvarez, for helping me gather several of said images; Jenny Berthiaume, who graciously gave me the "keys to the kingdom" of Badgeville's internal documentation; Tony Ventrice, for his extensive input on the subject of gamification in general and frameworks in particular, as well as for his efforts as a tech editor; Anita Flad, for making the necessary arrangements for me to hang in the Badgeville offices for a spell; Adena DeMonte, for her help with the final chapter in the book; and Havy Nguyen, Steve Sims, Tim Piatenko, Chris Duskin, Caroline Dangson, Paul Reeves, and Robin Krieglstein, for their willingness to share their extensive knowledge on various facets of gamification. Really, you guys rock!

In addition, several people at Wiley were instrumental to the publication of this title. First, thanks to my acquisitions editor, Stacy Kennedy, who was so gracious in giving me the opportunity to work on this project. In addition, my development editor, Corbin Collins, not only helped me usher this book from brain to page, he was a joy to work with. Thanks, too, to my proofreader, Evelyn Wellborn, who saved my bacon more than a few times. And thanks to Wiley's excellent production and composition staff. You guys are major pros!

Finally, I want to thank from the bottom of my heart my amazing family, who I not only love but like: my beautiful daughter, Heidi; my beloved partner in life, Olivier; my wonderful parents, Barb and Steve Shoup; my beautiful sister and specimen-like brother-in law, Jenny and Jim; my adorable nephew, Jake; and of course, Fergus the dog. I love you all like crazy.

— Kate Shoup

Publisher's Acknowledgments

We're proud of this book; please send us your comments at http://dummies.custhelp.com. For other comments, please contact our Customer Care Department within the U.S. at 877-762-2974, outside the U.S. at 317-572-3993, or fax 317-572-4002.

Some of the people who helped bring this book to market include the following:

Acquisitions, Editorial, and Vertical Websites

Editor: Corbin Collins

Acquisitions Editor: Stacy Kennedy

Assistant Editor: David Lutton

Editorial Program Coordinator: Joe Niesen

Technical Editors: Tony Ventrice

General Reviewer: Chris Lynch

Senior Editorial Manager: Jennifer Ehrlich

Editorial Manager: Carmen Krikorian

Editorial Assistants: Rachelle Amick and Alexa Koschier

Cover Photos: © Alexander Shirokov/ iStockPhoto.com

Cartoons: Rich Tennant (www.the5thwave.com)

Composition Services

Project Coordinator: Katie Crocker

Layout and Graphics: Carl Byers, Jennifer Creasey

Proofreaders: Lindsay Amones, Evelyn Wellborn

Indexer: BIM Indexing & Proofreading Services

Publishing and Editorial for Consumer Dummies

Kathleen Nebenhaus, Vice President and Executive Publisher

David Palmer, Associate Publisher

Kristin Ferguson-Wagstaffe, Product Development Director

Publishing for Technology Dummies

Andy Cummings, Vice President and Publisher

Composition Services

Debbie Stailey, Director of Composition Services

Contents at a Glance

Table of Contents

Part III: Getting Your Gamification Program Off the Ground.. 173

Chapter 10: Choosing a Gamification Provider...................175

Chapter 11: Key Expertise for Your Gamification Team 187

Chapter 12: Ready, Set, Go! Configuring and Deploying Gamification Elements.............................193

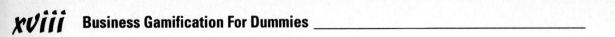

Introduction

Welcome to *Business Gamification For Dummies*!

Does this sound like you? Your organization has low retention or dismal conversion rates. Your customer communities are ghost towns. Your loyalty program is stagnant. Sometimes, it feels like customers have forgotten about your brand altogether.

Or maybe one of these problems is more familiar: Your employee onboarding process is slow as molasses. Your people don't collaborate. You have an employee churn rate higher than Mt. McKinley. Folks just don't perform — a problem that isn't helped by the fact that your expectations of employees have increased over time, and the systems you expect your employees to use have become more complicated.

The truth is, all these problems stem from a single cause: lack of engagement. In fact, lack of engagement — whether among customers or employees — can really do a number on your organization. On the customer side, customers who aren't engaged tend toward disloyalty; with ample choice, they fraternize with your competitors as much as (or more than) they do with you. And on the employee side, folks just don't perform.

Wouldn't it be the bee's knees if you could find some way to engage these people so they start performing the behaviors you want them to perform? Well, we have good news for you. You *can*. With gamification.

Gamification enables you to drive, measure, and reward high-value behaviors, whether by customers or employees. Game mechanics leverage design and behavioral psychology principles inherent in today's social games to drive and reward specific user behaviors in business environments. You can employ smart gamification elements — such as points, achievements, levels, leaderboards, missions, and contests — to drive desired behaviors on virtually any website or enterprise application. Gamification is less about games and more about figuring out what motivates people to perform — not to mention turning the mundane into the *fun*dane.

This book is your entrée into the wide world of gamification. In it, you'll discover how gamification works, what tools it uses, and how effective it can be at improving business for you. Are you ready to get started? If so, game on!

About This Book

Above all, *Business Gamification For Dummies* is a reference tool. You don't have to read it from beginning to end; instead, you can turn to any part of the book that gives you the information you need when you need it. And you can keep coming back to the book over and over. If you prefer to read things in order, you'll find that the information is presented in a natural, logical progression.

Conventions Used in This Book

To help you navigate this book, we include the following conventions:

- ✔ **Boldface** highlights key words in bulleted lists.
- ✔ New terms and words are emphasized in *italics*.
- ✔ Web addresses appear in `monofont`.

When this book was printed, some of the web addresses we mention may have broken across two lines of text. If that happened, rest assured that we didn't include any extra characters (such as hyphens) to indicate the break. If you want to visit a website whose URL has been broken, just type exactly what you see in this book, as though the line break didn't exist.

Foolish Assumptions

When writing this book, we generally assumed that readers were interested primarily in learning the ins and out of gamifying digital properties — websites, apps, and so on — rather than real-world ones. Although we do discuss applying gamification principles to events such as conferences and the like, and we touch on the ways real-world problems can be solved through broader gamification principles, our main focus is on the gamification of zeros-and-ones type environments.

We also assume to a degree that readers are more interested in low-cost or even no-cost rewards — think virtual rewards (which, when used correctly, can be as powerful if not more powerful than monetary rewards) — than monetary-based rewards. (You'll learn more about the various types of rewards in Chapter 5.)

How This Book Is Organized

Business Gamification For Dummies is organized into four parts, and the parts are divided into chapters. This section gives you a quick preview of what to expect from each part so you can turn to the part that interests you most.

Part 1: Basic Training: Grasping the Basics

As you embark on your gamification education, you'll quickly discover just how easy it is to get overwhelmed. The focus of this part is to inoculate you against gamification-related anxiety. In Chapter 1, you'll find out just what all the gamification fuss is about. In Chapter 2, you'll delve into the psychology of your users to find out what makes them tick. Chapter 3 is devoted to helping you pinpoint your business objectives, and Chapter 4 helps you determine what behaviors are likely to drive those objectives. In Chapter 5, you'll discover the importance of rewarding users, as well as what types of rewards are available to you. And in Chapter 6, you'll explore the various game mechanics employed in gamification. With these gamification basics under your belt, you'll be primed to use gamification to its fullest potential!

Part 11: Decisions, Decisions: Choosing a Gamification Framework

Regardless of whether you want to use gamification to increase customer engagement or encourage collaboration among employees, your next step is to determine just *how* to implement gamification. To aid in this, we've identified six gamification frameworks — holistic programs designed to achieve a specific business objective. Chapter 7 provides you with an overview of each framework — social loyalty, community expert, competitive pyramid, gentle guide, company collaborator, and company challenge — comparing and contrasting them. Chapters 8 and 9 offer more details on each of these frameworks in turn. Although you are not bound to use any one of these frameworks, gaining an understanding of them can help you assemble your own gamification program.

Part 111: Getting Your Gamification Program Off the Ground

In this part, you get practical advice on how to get your gamification program off the ground. Chapter 10 provides the 411 on whether to build your own gamification program from scratch or partner with a provider. You'll also get solid info on which providers are out there, at the ready. In Chapter 11, you discover exactly who belongs on your gamification team; Chapter 12 covers the basics of configuring and deploying your program. Chapter 13 is all about analytics, providing just the tip of the iceberg in terms of what kind of data you can gather with gamification. Finally, Chapter 14 offers a glimpse of where gamification may be heading from here on out.

Part IV: The Part of Tens

In this part, we offer our (admittedly unsolicited) opinions on good books for further reading as well as sites and apps that get gamification right. Chapter 15 features a list of excellent books covering more about gamification and related topics, such as reputation systems, as well as the larger topics of motivation, persuasion, change, habits, and human behavior. If you're ready to expand your knowledge in these fascinating areas, get reading! Chapter 16 offers a look at several sites that feature smart gamification. Oh, and there's also an appendix that shows you how to supercharge your sales teams with gamification.

Icons Used in This Book

Icons are those little pictures you see in the margins throughout this book, and they're meant to draw your attention to key points that help you along the way. Here's a list of the icons we use and what they signify.

Some things are so important, they need to be set apart for emphasis. This icon — like a string tied around your finger — is a friendly reminder of stuff to commit to memory and use over the long haul.

When you see this icon in the margin, the paragraph next to it contains a valuable, practical tip about using gamification.

This icon highlights things you want to avoid. An important part of achieving success is simply eliminating the mistakes; the information marked by this icon helps you do just that.

This icon highlights information that may be interesting if you want to really drill down to another level of technicality, but that can be safely skipped without jeopardizing your understanding of the topic at hand.

Sidebars

Sometimes, we have information we want to share with you, but it relates only tangentially to the topic at hand. When that happens, we put that information in a sidebar. Even though it may not be mission-critical, we think you'll still find it worth knowing.

Where to Go from Here

Glance through the table of contents or index and find the part, chapter, or section that flips your switch. That's usually the best place to begin. If you're just trying to get a sense of what gamification is about, you'll want to start with the chapters in Part I. If you kind of already know something about gamification and are ready to look at some of your options and how they might work, check out Part II. If you're itching to get going and launch your own gamification program, Part III is ready to step you through the process of building it. If your program is up and running but you're a little unsure about the analytics side of the equation, you'll want to flip right to Chapter 13.

After you've finished reading this book, you'll want to invest some time considering your business objectives, the behaviors most likely to drive those objectives, and the mechanics most likely to drive those behaviors. With that information in hand, you're well on your way to developing a gamification program.

Play on!

Part I

Basic Training:
Grasping
the Basics

The 5th Wave   By Rich Tennant

"This company really values its customers.
I just leveled up to be their CEO."

In this part . . .

As you embark on your gamification education, it's easy to get overwhelmed. This part is devoted to helping you stave off any gamification-related anxiety. In addition to discovering what all the fuss is about, you'll find out just what makes your users tick and consider what business objectives you want to achieve through gamification. We help you determine what types of behaviors might drive those objectives, and you'll explore the various types of rewards available for your program. Finally, you'll survey the game mechanics common in many programs. With these basics under your belt, you'll be primed to use gamification to its fullest potential.

Chapter 1

Gamifi-wha? Introducing Gamification

*G*amification. Say the word, and chances are the response will be, "Gamifi-wha?" It's not even in the dictionary — meaning, ironically, that you can't use it in a game of *Words with Friends*.

The fact is, the term just hasn't made it to the mainstream vernacular — although we're confident it soon will. Before August 2010, almost no one searched for the term *gamification* on Google. Starting in January 2011, however, searches have spiked. And according to Gartner, Inc., by 2014, more than 70 percent of Global 2000 organizations will have at least one gamified application. Some experts project that the gamification market will grow to $2.8 billion by 2016!

In this chapter, you'll find out what gamification is, how it works, and who's using it. You'll also discover the basic steps involved in launching a gamification program.

Although the word *gamification* may be new, games themselves are not. Far from it! Indeed, games have been played for millennia. Witness the 3,000-year-old set of dice unearthed at an archaeological site in Iran, and the fact that people in China have been playing Go since about the same time. Games are an integral part of all societies the world over.

Paging Mr. Webster: Defining Gamification

So what does gamification mean? Simply put, *gamification* refers to the use of game mechanics and rewards in a non-game setting to increase user engagement and drive desired user behaviors. (You'll learn all about rewards in Chapter 5, and game mechanics in Chapter 6.) You can use gamification to increase such things as stickiness, sharing, content creation, purchases, and so on.

Best behavior

In part, the idea behind gamification is to tap into people's innate desire to play games to influence how they behave and what they do. (This innate desire explains why games are big business. In 2010 alone, digital games generated $25 billion in sales.) It's about making things fun — something that game makers have known for decades, but that the rest of us are just figuring out.

More than that, though, gamification is about tapping into what really motivates people and then using a variety of techniques (discussed throughout the book) to inspire them to perform desired behaviors. As an added bonus, with gamification, the desired behaviors that users perform are recordable — and when you have data, you have an opportunity to act on it.

Sound creepy? Fair point well made. Yes, gamification can certainly be used to promote behaviors in which people might not otherwise engage. But the best gamification programs operate by rewarding people for behaviors they are already inclined to perform or are required to perform, increasing their engagement and enjoyment. In other words, gamification makes things more fun.

If you're feeling skeptical, consider this: If you've tucked a frequent shopper card in your wallet in the hopes of someday getting one free sub, purchased a plane ticket using airline miles, been Employee of the Month, or earned your black belt in karate, you've already seen the effects of gamification. All those are real-world examples of gamification in action. Honestly, if you think about it, this type of gamification is everywhere — and it has been for a while. What's new is that gamification is now being applied to websites and software applications. That's the kind we focus on in this book.

This book strives to teach you to apply gamification techniques to every facet of your business, to help you meet your business goals.

To be clear, gamification isn't about creating a game. Don't get us wrong — games are great. But slapping a game on your site probably won't help you attract more users. Rather, with gamification, you use game mechanics to enliven an existing experience — say, a community-based website, an employee training program, or a weight-loss program — making it more fun and engaging.

Real-world gamification examples

Want to see some other examples of real-world gamification? Visit `www. thefuntheory.com`. An initiative of Volkswagen, the site is dedicated to changing people's behavior for the better by, well, making things more fun. Examples include a seat belt that's fun to use; a bottle bank arcade machine to boost recycling efforts; a speed camera lottery that enters drivers who are obeying the speed limit into a lottery, funded by fines collected from speeders; a "piano staircase," which lights up and plays sounds to encourage people to bypass the escalator; and the "world's deepest bin," a trash can that uses sound effects to create the illusion that the bin is insanely deep, to encourage people not to litter.

Volkswagen isn't the only organization trying to solve problems by making things more fun. Another great example comes from the University of Washington, where researchers have developed Foldit, an online puzzle that enables people — anyone, including you — to contribute to important science research simply by playing. Has it been successful? Well, if you call gamers discovering in 10 days how a key protein may help cure HIV— something scientists had been researching for 15 years — successful, then yes, the game has been successful. (See *Time*'s website for a nifty article on this amazing result: `http://techland.time.com/2011/09/19/foldit-gamers-solve-aids-puzzle-that-baffled-scientists-for-decade`.)

Similar movements, called *serious game* movements, are percolating in other areas, too: military training, corporate training, first-responder training, civilization simulations, ecology simulations, public-policy campaigns, and more. All these serve as further examples of gamification.

What Gamification Does

Does your organization have low retention or dismal conversion rates? Are your customer communities ghost towns? Is your loyalty program stagnant? Have customers forgotten your brand altogether?

Or maybe your problems are on the employee side of the equation. It could be that your onboarding process for getting new employees set up is slow. Or maybe your people just don't collaborate, share knowledge, or keep records the way they should. Maybe you have a high employee churn rate.

All these problems stem from a single cause: lack of engagement. The fact is, lack of engagement — whether among customers or employees — can really do a number on your organization.

Here are two ways lack of engagement can hurt:

✔ **Customers aren't loyal.** The Internet has leveled the playing field, inundating customers with choices. Thanks to this ample choice, they often flee to competitors.

✔ **Employees under perform.** Under utilizing the technology you provide, employees fail to optimize business processes.

In response, most organizations have simply invested in more technology — lots of it. Like, $1 trillion (that's *trillion*, with a *t*) between 2007 and 2012 alone. Even so, here's the stubborn reality:

✔ 54 percent of customers are inactive in loyalty programs.

✔ 69 percent of customers don't use online communities.

✔ 50 percent of employees don't adopt enterprise software.

✔ 88 percent of employees don't use social software.

What's missing? Simple. Your ability to measure and influence behaviors that matter to you. Enter gamification.

Gamification enables you to drive, measure, and reward high-value behaviors by customers or employees. Game mechanics leverage design and behavioral psychology principles inherent in today's social games to drive and reward specific user behaviors in business environments. Smart gamification elements — such as points, achievements, levels, leaderboards, missions, and contests — can be employed to drive desired behaviors on virtually any website or enterprise application (see Figure 1-1).

Your customers and employees, like anyone, crave attention, recognition, approval, and rewards. With gamification, you feed this craving and in the process convert customers into loyal fans and employees into highly effective collaborators and advocates.

Gamification: The intersection of psychology and technology

One way to think of gamification is as the intersection of psychology and technology. Most successful gamification programs rely to some degree on behavioral psychology — understanding what motivates someone to engage with certain elements on a website, app, or what have you.

In the past, the people who designed websites and software applications were concerned with simply developing technology — say, to automate a business process or to make it more streamlined. They weren't so worried about making sure people would actually *use*

it. Nowadays, it's about humanizing the technology and applying psychological and behavioral concepts to increase the likelihood that the technology will be used and used properly.

It's a little like ergonomics. Sure, there were hammers before. But when someone thought to shape the handle so it was easier to grasp, and to add rubber to make the handle grippy, so it wouldn't slip, suddenly the hammer became easier and more pleasurable to use. Similarly, technology designed with psychological and behavioral concepts in mind is simply more delicious.

Figure 1-1:
With gamification, you can drive desired behaviors across your technology investments to get the value you wanted.

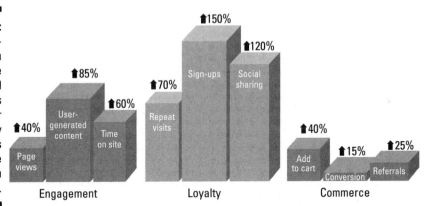

Illustration by Wiley, Composition Services Graphics

People *really* crave recognition, and their reputations are important to them. Gamification enables you to tap into those motivating forces. When done correctly, it's amazingly effective.

Proof Positive: Does Gamification Work?

Yes, gamification works. Next question.

Oh — you want evidence. Fair enough. Here are a few specific examples:

- ✔ **Beat the GMAT (BTG):** The world's largest social network for MBA applicants, BTG launched a social network called MBA Watch as part of its effort to build a high-quality community of MBA candidates. In an attempt to motivate and influence users to share insights and knowledge techniques in solving problems, BTG used various gamification techniques, including badges and leaderboards. The results: A 195 percent increase in pages visited, a 370 percent increase on time spent on site, and 50,000 activities performed by 8,000 users.

- ✔ **Sneakpeeq:** This purveyor of up-and-coming style, home, and living brands sought to redefine the way people shop by gamifying its website. As users explore the site, they are awarded points for performing various specific behaviors, including sharing on Facebook or Twitter, *peeqing* at a product page to see a special price, and *loving* products. Top users at the end of each shopping day are rewarded with site credit, which they can redeem at any Sneakpeeq store. The results: a 70 percent month-over-month lift in *peeqs*, a 590 percent lift in social shares, a 935 percent lift in loves, and a 3,000 percent lift in buy clicks.

- ✔ **Interscope Records:** This American record label, which manages dozens of artists and bands, sought to encourage people who visited its websites to post, comment, watch videos, share content, and perform other high-value behaviors. By applying smart gamification, Interscope enabled a 40 percent increase in comments, an 18 percent increase in shares, and a whopping 650 percent increase in engagement.

- ✔ **MuchMusic.com:** MuchMusic, the Canadian equivalent to MTV, received millions of visitors each year on its website, MuchMusic.com. But Much needed a way to foster more repeat visits. Enter gamification. Using game mechanics, Much began rewarding visitors for performing such actions as signing up, leaving a comment, uploading content, voting on polls, and so on. The company also devised various missions to generate engagement with specific shows and campaigns. The results: In the first month, more than 23,000 users created accounts on the site — a 21 percent increase, with nearly one in three returning on a daily basis. In addition, more than 325,000 behaviors were rewarded, and nearly 120,000 achievements unlocked.

All that being said, gamification is not necessarily a panacea. If your business or product is lousy, or if you're at the bottom of a dying industry, gamification alone can't save you. It's a little like the lipstick-on-a-pig analogy. No matter how much lipstick you put on a pig, it's still a pig in lipstick. At the end of the day, people look for value. If your value proposition sucks, gamification can't make it suck less.

Remember the old slogan of BASF, the German chemical company? "At BASF, we don't make a lot of the products you buy. We make a lot of the products you buy better." That's kind of what gamification does. It doesn't make your offering; it makes your offering *better*.

Who's on First: Who's Using Gamification?

So what are some of the industries that are already using gamification? Here are just a few:

- Retail and e-commerce
- Politics
- Healthcare
- Nonprofit
- Human resources

World-class retailers, e-commerce communities, and consumer brands — including Footlocker, Samsung, Bluefly, Barnes & Noble, General Mills, and Dannon — rely on gamification to meet key business objectives.

Gamification in politics

In an attempt to engage constituents of varying age groups, some political campaigns have begun to tap into gamification. For example, during the 2012 presidential campaign, Barack Obama's campaign website (www.barackobama.com) ran a contest— the prize: dinner with the president and First Lady — to persuade site visitors to donate. Perhaps an even more overt example was the Obama campaign's G.O.P. Debate Watch site (www.gopdebatewatch.com), where Democratic supporters could play a game in which they pledged to donate each time a Republican candidate used a word from a pre-designated "hot list" during the debate (think *Obamacare*, *flat tax*, *socialism*, and so on). Gamification is also used by political campaigns to foster competition among canvassers — in a fun way.

North Carolina Governor Beverly Perdue took gamification of politics to a whole new level with the launch of her Balance the Budget Challenge, a game, complete with a friendly dog character, in which players must find the right mix of choices to get the state's deficit to zero (see Figure 1-2). Numbers are based on real data, and the proposals included in the game — which pertain to education, social services, public safety, general government, jobs, and more — are the very same proposals the governor herself had to entertain when preparing her own budget.

Figure 1-2:
North
Carolina's
Balance
the Budget
Challenge.

Image courtesy of the State of North Carolina

Gamification in healthcare

Healthcare is one area where gamification has really taken off. Indeed, loads of health insurers, including UnitedHealth Group, BlueCross BlueShield, and Aetna, have launched initiatives to gamify their offerings. For example, Aetna's online social game, Mindbloom, helps members improve health and wellness and lead a more balanced life.

In addition, several startups have emerged, using gamification in an attempt to make fitness more fun. Here are just a few:

✔ Nike+ (http://nikeplus.nike.com/plus) enables members to track activities, compare results, set goals, and improve performance — as well as receive training tips and tricks from world-class coaches. Games, challenges, and virtual competitions with friends help users stay inspired.

✔ With Fitocracy's free iPhone app (downloadable from `www.fitocracy.com`), users can log their workouts and receive points for them. As they do, they earn achievements and badges, as well as take on new challenges. Engagement is further promoted through the use of social tools. For example, users can add friends, join groups, follow others, chat, comment, and compare results.

✔ GymPact (`www.gym-pact.com`) helps members stick to their workouts by rewarding them with cash when they do — paid for by members who fail to work out as promised.

✔ With HealthRally (`www.heathrally.com`), members can reward friends or family members for meeting fitness goals, or ask friends and family members to reward them.

✔ A service called EveryMove (`www.everymove.org`), currently in beta, will enable members to earn rewards such as discounts on health insurance by achieving health goals.

Gamification in nonprofit

The nonprofit world has used gamification to great effect to build awareness of critical causes and increase engagement.

Movember, an organization that promotes awareness of prostate cancer and other male-related cancers, is perhaps best known for its annual mustache-based fundraising challenge in November of each year. Movember motivates its 'stache-growers by issuing clever challenges and offering big rewards, including the highly coveted International Man of Movember.

Gamification in HR

Human resources officials in several organizations have begun to use gamification to recruit and motivate employees. For example, in an effort to motivate senior executives to complete its leadership development program, Deloitte has gamified its Deloitte Leadership Academy, a program that delivers lessons from world-renowned business schools (such as Harvard, Stanford, and so on). As participants complete programs, contribute, and share knowledge, they earn badges and other rewards — which are portable to sites like LinkedIn and Twitter.

A more extreme example might be Marriott, which went so far as to develop a FarmVille-style, Facebook-based game called My Marriott Hotel in which players juggle the duties of a hotel kitchen manager. The idea is to acquaint young workers with the industry in the hopes of recruiting them. This goes beyond mere gamification to the creation of an actual game.

Developing a Gamification Program

Interested in applying gamification to *your* business? If so, the first thing you need to recognize is that just as losing weight involves a lifestyle change, not just a diet, gamification is a program, not just a project.

You can't just apply gamification for three months and call it a day; you need to invest in the strategy for the long term.

The next sections discuss the steps involved in developing a gamification program. These steps are as follows:

- ✔ Pinpointing your business objectives
- ✔ Identifying the user behaviors that will drive your business objectives
- ✔ Choosing rewards
- ✔ Selecting game mechanics
- ✔ Choosing a framework
- ✔ Deciding whether to build or buy your gamification system and choosing a provider
- ✔ Assembling your gamification team
- ✔ Configuring and deploying your gamification program
- ✔ Using analytics to track your progress

Pinpointing your business objectives

Yes, it's tempting to just slap some game mechanics on your company's website and call it a day. But gamifying your business is, unfortunately, a bit more complicated. For your gamification efforts to be successful, you must first pinpoint your business objectives — what, exactly, you want to achieve.

Maybe you want to increase customer engagement. Maybe you want to build a community around your website. Or perhaps you want to improve employee performance. After you've identified what, exactly, you want to achieve, you can design a gamification program that helps you meet that goal. You'll learn more about defining your business objectives in Chapter 3.

Identifying desired behaviors

Next you have to determine which user behaviors will drive the objectives you identified. Put simply, behaviors are the foundation of all gamification programs. Once key behaviors are identified, you can determine which game mechanics are most likely to drive those behaviors and reward users for performing those behaviors — that's what gamification is all about. For more on identifying key behaviors, see Chapter 4.

Choosing rewards

Even the mere *hope* of receiving a reward — even a really lousy one — can motivate a player to perform a desired behavior. It makes sense, then, that successful gamification hinges on the use of rewards (preferably good ones). Rewards can be divided into three categories: recognition (in the form of reputation or status), privileges (for example, early access to products or site features, moderation powers, or stronger votes), and monetary rewards (think discounts, free shipping, prizes, or redemptions). For help deciding which type of reward is right for your program, read Chapter 5.

Selecting game mechanics

Game mechanics describes the components of a game — the tools employed by game designers to generate and reward activity among players (or, in the case of a gamification program, customers, employees, or other users). Most gamification programs leverage game mechanics in one way or another. When it comes to game mechanics, various tools are available to you, each designed to elicit a specific reaction from players. These tools, which can be combined in infinite ways to create a broad spectrum of responses and experiences, include points, leaderboards (see Figure 1-3), levels, missions, challenges, quests, achievements, rewards, and feedback. You'll learn more about all these game mechanics in Chapter 6.

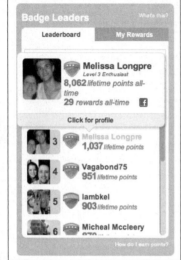

Figure 1-3: Leaderboards are one example of effective game mechanics.

Image courtesy of Badgeville

Choosing a framework

A *gamification framework* is a holistic program designed to achieve a specific business objective. The framework you use depends on the outcome you want to achieve. Each framework — we've identified six of them — is designed to tackle a specific business need.

Some of these frameworks address an internal (*employee-facing*) need, while others are designed for external (*customer-facing*) use. Some frameworks work best in solo environments (for an individual); others are ideal for collaborative settings (for example, a community); and still others speak to competitive arenas (say, a gaming site).

The six gamification frameworks we've identified are as follows:

- ✔ **Social loyalty:** This framework is for customer-facing experiences that occur in non-social environments, such as a traditional e-commerce experience. It focuses on rewards.

- ✔ **Community expert:** This framework is for customer-facing experiences that rely on quality user-generated content and contributions. It focuses on reputation.

✔ **Competitive pyramid:** This framework is for customer-facing communities that seek to motivate competitive behavior. It focuses on status and score.

✔ **Gentle guide:** This framework guides employees through a process. It focuses on ensuring completion and compliance.

✔ **Company collaborator:** This framework is designed to increase contributions by employees, developers, and partners in internal communities.

✔ **Company challenge:** This framework is designed to challenge your staff to compete on teams to encourage various behaviors, which are tracked in internal business systems.

The chapters in Part II cover all six of these frameworks in detail.

Deciding to build or buy, and choosing a provider

Should you attempt to build your gamification program in house from the ground up? Or should you buy a gamification system from a company that specializes in that sort of thing? That's a decision you'll need to make as you develop your gamification program. For guidance, see Chapter 10.

Assembling your gamification team

Regardless of whether you build your gamification program in house or partner with a gamification provider, you'll want to assemble a top-notch team to see it through. Some team members might be employees in your organization. Others could be external — say, consultants from a gamification provider or other third party. Broadly speaking, these team members will include business champions, nerds, and creative types. For more, see Chapter 11.

Configuring and deploying your gamification program

It probably goes without saying that gamification programs can be quite complex. But don't freak out! When you break it down, it really consists of just four simple stages:

1. Design

2. Development

3. Testing

4. Migration

You'll read about the ins and outs of each of these stages in Chapter 12.

Using analytics to track your progress

How do you know that the gamification program you put in place is actually driving the behaviors you need to occur in order to meet your business objectives? Analytics. Using analytics, you can assess the success (or lack thereof) of any business operation. With analytics, you can pinpoint where the problems with your program lie — Is the design off somehow? Did you use the wrong platform? — and determine how to correct them. In today's high-tech world, it's all about optimization, and that's exactly what analytics allows you to do. For more on analytics, see Chapter 13.

Chapter 2

Head Case: Understanding What Makes Users Tick

In This Chapter
▶ Identifying types of players
▶ Understanding extrinsic versus intrinsic motivators
▶ Distinguishing competition and cooperation
▶ Identifying things people like
▶ Noting key behavior motivators

*I*f your business objective involves persuading a consumer or an employee to take some type of action — say, becoming a registered user or filling out a form — then it behooves you to gain some understanding of what makes people tick. Indeed, understanding player motivation is key to designing a successful gamification system. And that, in turn, increases the chances of meeting your business objective.

The more you know about what motivates your target audience, the more likely it is that you'll be able to design a gamification system that drives their behavior in just the right way.

Just Your Type: Identifying Player Types

You may be wondering: Why are people motivated by game mechanics in the first place? Lots of reasons:

✔ The sheer pleasure of mastery

✔ Rank, status, or reputation within a community

✔ A desire to de-stress

✔ A need to socialize

✔ To have fun

Just as there are many reasons for playing games, there are various types of players — four, if you ask game scholar Richard Bartle. (He's somewhat of a smarty-pants, having earned a PhD in artificial intelligence from England's University of Essex.) Some players are more focused on other players; some are more interested in the game world itself. Similarly, some players tend toward action, whereas others are more about interaction (see Figure 2-1). Understanding these four player types can help you design gamification programs that are more interesting to your users.

According to Bartle, the four player types are as follows:

✔ **Explorers:** An explorer is just what you'd think: a player who likes to explore and dig around the game. For the explorer, the experience itself is the objective rather than, say, accumulating points or earning badges. Explorers are particularly keen on rich environments; the more nooks and crannies, the better.

✔ **Achievers:** Born competitors, achievers will go to great lengths to accumulate points and prestige. Unlike explorers, who are content to toodle around in the game environment, achievers favor scenarios in which they're rewarded for completing tasks. Earning the recognition of others is also important to achievers.

✔ **Socializers:** Unlike achievers, whose focus is on accumulating points and prestige, socializers are more interested in the social interaction that is an integral part of game play. That's not to say that socializers don't care about winning and whatnot — they do. They just care *more* about the socializing. Not surprisingly, socializers have lots of friends, making them particularly valuable to organizations interested in gamification.

✔ **Killers:** Killers are in it to win it. Killers don't care if other players like them; they care only that other players respect them.

Killers are an integral part of any competitive game. However, you must resist the temptation to design a gamification experience exclusively for this player type. Doing so is sure to alienate anyone who doesn't fit in this category.

Actually, we lied. Bartle has since identified more than four player types — eight more, to be exact. These are friend, griefer, hacker, networker, opportunist, planner, politician, and scientist. That being said, the four player types listed here are the ones you *really* need to know about.

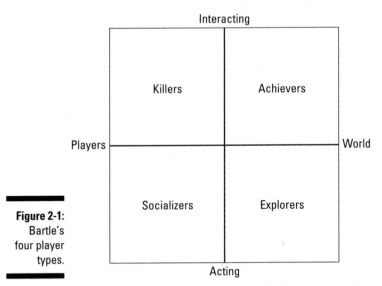

Illustration by Wiley, Composition Services Graphics, based on an image by Bartle

Figure 2-1:
Bartle's
four player
types.

In general, people aren't exclusively one player type or another. Most people exhibit each player type in varying degrees.

Although your gamification program won't be an actual game, understanding the different types of game players is important, as is applying those specific player types to your customers and employees to drive desired behaviors. As mentioned, some customers and employees will be motivated to help each other or be acknowledged for their engagement, whereas others will be motivated to compete.

Outie or Innie? Understanding Extrinsic Versus Intrinsic Motivators

A key aspect of just about any behavior is *motivation* — why someone does what he does. A person may be motivated by any number of things: a desire for status or money, to help others, to find meaning in life — or simply to express himself.

Those who study psychology place people's motivations in one of two categories:

✔ **Extrinsic motivations:** These are rewards that come from outside. Want to win a gold medal in the Olympics? That's an external motivation. Ditto the desire to drive a fancy car or lose those last ten pounds. Of course, the most prominent extrinsic motivation is money. Every paid job in the world has an extrinsic motivation, be it salary, tips, commission, benefits, stock options, bribes, table scraps, or some combination thereof. An argument could also be made that power (or authority) is an extrinsic motivation.

✔ **Intrinsic motivations:** Intrinsic motivations are motivations that come from within. Intrinsic rewards are things that make you *feel* good. For example, suppose you enjoy painting watercolors, and you merely want to improve your skills. That's an example of an intrinsic motivation. You don't want to become a better painter so you can be a world-famous artist; you simply want, for your own personal reasons, to improve your painting because you enjoy painting. With intrinsic motivation, the result is often growth — growth as an intellectual journey, growth due to challenges overcome, growth due to a broadening of your social connections, and growth due to the creation of order.

Intrinsic motivators are meaningful. They include things like developing a sense of

✔ Identity

✔ Self-expression

✔ Status

✔ Place in a community

✔ Progress and direction

✔ Accomplishment

Generally, people view intrinsic motivation as being "better" — perhaps more *noble* — than extrinsic motivation. Intrinsic motivators, they say, foster greatness, whereas extrinsic motivators foster greed. Indeed, recent research has shown that in modern life, intrinsic motivators can be more powerful than extrinsic ones.

Although it's true that the holy grail of any gamification program is to foster intrinsically motivated behaviors, anyone who's ever watched a rat in a cage knows food pellets — an extrinsic reward — can be pretty persuasive, too. Sure, it may be possible to drive a rat's behavior using some other, more intrinsic method, but you can't deny that the pellets do the job. The bottom line? Fostering intrinsically motivated behavior is great, and fostering extrinsically motivated behaviors is okay. Ideally, you'll do both if you can. Just don't ignore the intrinsic, even if it's harder to see.

Dangers of extrinsic motivators

Although your gamification program can certainly use extrinsic motivators, you must be aware that doing so can upset the balance. For example, suppose the people who visit your site aren't particularly inclined to share information about their site activity on Facebook. You, however, want them to do so, and you encourage the behavior by awarding 10 points per share — more than you give for any other behavior.

Now imagine you have two users, Angus and Fergus. Angus is a dedicated member of your site. He loves viewing content and leaving comments, but he's not big into posting to Facebook. In contrast, Fergus is a casual member of the site. He likes its gamification features, and his mission in life is to outscore everyone else. What do you suppose might happen? You guessed it. Fergus will post anything and everything on Facebook to increase his score as quickly as possible and will shoot right to the top of the leaderboard. In contrast, Angus — your more dedicated user — may become upset by and lose interest in the gamification program, and may even visit your site less.

To make matters worse, your site will probably have gained little benefit from Fergus's increased Facebook activity. Odds are, his friends blocked or ignored his post after the first few spammed his feed. Indeed, they might even have developed a negative impression of your website in the process.

The limitations of extrinsic rewards don't have to be the end to your gamification agenda. Once those extrinsic rewards are understood, they actually become a wonderful lens with which to view your customers and employees. The more you understand what motivates your users, the stronger their relationship with your company will be.

The Fogg Behavior Model

Noted innovator, social scientist, and teacher Dr. BJ Fogg, founder and director of the Persuasive Technology Lab at Stanford University, has developed what he calls the Fogg Behavior Model. According to this model, three elements must converge in order for a behavior to occur:

- **Trigger:** The event that prompts a behavior (or not).
- **Motivation:** Why someone does what he or she does. This might include sensation, anticipation, social cohesion, and so on.
- **Ability:** The power to do something. Factors in ability include time, money, knowledge, physical effort, mental effort, and so on. The more able a person is to perform the desired behavior, the more likely he or she is to do so.

Here's an example: Remember in *When Harry Met Sally* when Sally, played by Meg Ryan, refuses to answer a call from Harry? Harry, played by Billy Crystal, leaves her a message on her answering machine, saying, "The fact that you're not answering leads me to believe you're either (a) not at home, (b) at home but don't want to talk to me, or (c) home, desperately want to talk to me, but trapped under something heavy." This scene hits on all major points in the Fogg Behavior Model: the trigger (a — the ringing phone), (b) motivation, and (c) ability.

Note that if motivation is low (b) and ability is low (c), then even if a trigger occurs (the phone rings), the desired behavior (answering the phone) will likely not transpire. In contrast, if both motivation and ability are high, then chances are the desired behavior *will* occur as a result of the trigger. Interestingly, if motivation is high but ability is low (or vice versa), the behavior has a fighting chance of happening.

One more interesting note: According to Fogg, motivation may be overplayed. That is, we talk a lot about motivating behavior, but in fact, the low-hanging fruit is ability. After all, according to Fogg, increasing ability is just as effective as increasing motivation — and often easier to accomplish. In gamification terms, this low-hanging fruit might be improving your interface to make it easier to use or in training your users.

Competition Versus Cooperation

In assessing your audience, you'll want to consider whether they are competitive, cooperative, or some combination of the two. To be *competitive* is to have, according to *Merriam-Webster*, a "very strong desire to win or be the best at something." In contrast, being *cooperative* involves having "two or more people or groups working together to do something."You could argue that competitive players are likely killers, while cooperative players are more probably socializers.

To some extent, whether a person is more competitive or cooperative is culturally dependent. The West places great emphasis on competition — indeed, on winning at all costs. In contrast, many Eastern cultures find competition distasteful and emphasize cooperative behavior. This may be a consideration as you design your gamification system.

Interestingly, the gulf between competitive and cooperative behavior may not be as wide as one might imagine or as is often perceived. Indeed, the word "compete" stems from the Latin *competere*, meaning "to seek together." And although certain models of competition are decidedly cutthroat — particularly the military model, in which opponents are viewed as mortal enemies — others emphasize comradeship with teammates, coaches, and even opposing players.

Speaking of teammates — or, more specifically, of teams — they're a great motivational tool. Why? They bring the best of both worlds. Players enjoy the same thrill of victory as they would on their own, but less of the sting of defeat. That is, if you win, you feel great. And if you lose, that loss is distributed across the team so you don't feel quite so bad as if you had lost on your own. Teams also give the born leaders in your group a chance to show their stuff. You'll learn more about teams in Chapter 9.

As with player types, people are typically not purely competitive or cooperative but fall somewhere on a spectrum. Players on the competitive end of the spectrum are the ones most likely to be trolling for some type of competitive activity. Renowned psychologist Dr. John Houston, who specializes in studying competitive behavior, notes that "Competitive people have a very low threshold for when they will jump into a competition and are likely already seeking out ways to compete." That being said, catering exclusively to competitive, versus cooperative, players will ultimately reduce participation, as players on the cooperative side will likely be alienated and quit the game.

Key Club: Motivating Key Behaviors

It sounds absurdly simple, but one way to drive behavior is to harness game mechanics to enable people to experience something they like. Easy, right? Well, yes — until you consider the fact that the answer to the question "What do people like?" is as varied as people themselves. In general terms, here are just a few things people like:

- ✔ Recognition
- ✔ Status
- ✔ Identity
- ✔ Specialization

- Positive reinforcement
- Rewards
- Relevance
- Competition
- Visualization of progress
- Baby steps

Recognizing users

Who doesn't love to recognized? Pretty much no one, that's who. Which explains why recognition for achievement — be it in the form of badges, trophies, or general kudos — is part of just about every type of competition, games and otherwise, on Earth. On a site, that could mean being recognized for expertise based on writing reviews. Inside a company, it could be an achievement for closing more sales in your customer management software.

It's critical to let people know how much you appreciate them when they behave in a way that's important or valuable to your organization. That might be a simple thanks, a high five, a "like," or a vote — some type of visual cue that both conveys your appreciation to the person being recognized and shares that information with the community as a whole. Recognition for achieving a task or accomplishing a goal not only feeds human needs, but it encourages engagement and increases repetition.

Recognition is a foundational building block for gamification. Recognition simply means acknowledging desired behaviors. Everything else is either a *form* of recognition or a dynamic dependent on recognition.

Some people don't just want to be recognized; they want to be heroes. This desire is particularly prevalent among the male 18-35 year old demographic and is the driving force behind countless games. (Donkey Kong, in which a lowly plumber must rescue a princess from a gorilla, comes to mind.) In a gamification program, you can do this by rewarding people who are the first to respond to a key challenge. For example, if someone posts a question about a product, you could give whoever replies to that question first a First Responder badge.

A word on fame

Although one might think that fame is simply an extension of recognition for achievement, anyone who follows the Kardashians can tell you otherwise. That is, no actual achievement is necessary to attain fame. Rather, fame has to do with how many people, in the words of gamification evangelist Gabe Zichermann, "view, favor, subscribe, watch, talk about, tweet, or otherwise socially endorse someone." But fame in a gamification program isn't limited to celebrities; it's for people being rewarded for performing valuable behaviors within the context of their specific community. So, in the case of a company's intranet, everyday employees can be showcased for performing valuable behaviors that matter to them.

Conferring status

Unless you're an invertebrate, status is probably important to you. Indeed, for some users, status is everything. *Status* refers to a position or rank relative to others. Those with a higher position or rank are conferred a higher status. Within a social environment, relative position of an individual compared to others is important. Status — and the rewards or privileges that come with it — are valuable to the player because of the sense of worth and pride that comes with an increased standing in a community of their peers.

American Express is a great example of a company that uses status as a motivator. It offers green cards for regular members, a gold card for more well-off members, a platinum card for even wealthier members, and a special black card for your Donald Trump types. When an AmEx member hands over a black card to purchase an item, the person on the receiving end knows the buyer is a Big Deal.

In a gamified environment, status is less transactional. It's often tied to valuable behaviors that support a company's business objectives, regardless of whether it's based on an explicit transaction. On an electronics Web site, for example, you might reward a user who submits really high quality reviews. It doesn't matter that she doesn't spend as much at your site as other customers — she is championed among the user base because her contributions drive engagement.

Not surprisingly, status — represented by using many of the same tools as recognition for achievement — is an important element in many game systems. In a support community, an example could be becoming a Level 5 expert for your efforts in answering customer questions.

As users earn rewards for their behaviors and become more engaged via gamification, a natural byproduct is enhanced status, rank, and reputation. The recognition of expertise or knowledge within a community — coupled with the inherent competition involved in progressing through different levels of achievement — is a critical element of any gamification program.

Establishing identity

In the case of certain users, it's all about identity. They want to be known. Recognizing who a user is, what expertise he carries, and what social standing he has is important. Ideally, the distinguishing character or personality of an individual is also showcased, leading to desirable engagement and increased community participation.

Identifying specialization

Maybe your user knows everything there is to know about cloud computing. Or tying knots. Or going vegan. Or curling. Expertise in an area, or *specialization*, will typically cause users to perform actions that relate to that topic. For example, a vegan might start a thread on a forum about a new vegan product. A cloud-computing expert might generate a blog post on the topic. This in turn should help to build his or her reputation as an expert in that field.

Traditional tools convey people's expertise, or specialization, by enabling them to enter this information in editable profile fields. With gamification, however, expertise is identified through contextually relevant behaviors. It's based on what people actually *do*, not just what they *say* they're good at doing.

Pillars of reinforcement

There are a few different types of reinforcement or, as we like to call them — trumpets, please — the pillars of reinforcement. They are as follows:

✔ **Personal accomplishment:** Tracking progress and visualizing goals enable users to build a sense of personal accomplishment. This pillar involves the use of clear instructions, praise, and reassurance for making progress. People want constant reminders that their actions have purpose and that they are moving toward clearly defined goals. Gamification can provide an effective contrast to the ambiguous goals and irregular rewards of real life.

✔ **Social experience:** Users like to express identity and connect with like-minded individuals, fostering a stronger social experience. This is important for users who want to be part of a larger community. This pillar involves such things as cooperating, comparing, sharing, and listening. Possibly even more than they crave personal accomplishment, people want to feel like they belong. At the same time, they want to feel like they have a unique identity. Building social experiences involves giving users the tools to compare and contrast their thoughts, personalities, and behaviors.

✔ **Competition:** Competition is a special form of social experience where progress is subjective and the community is clearly ranked. There is a "best" and a "worst," and everyone knows where on that scale they stand. When it works, competition is incredibly powerful; any activity that can get your heart racing can become addictive. But for this very reason it can also fail — the stress of failure can be too much for casual users looking to relax.

After reading about these three pillars, you're probably thinking that your site needs them all. And you're right. Assuming you have unlimited resources and unlimited time to tune and tweak, you can't go wrong with all three. But resources aren't unlimited, meaning you'll probably need to be strategic about which ones you use. The smart choice is to identify the one pillar that most resonates with your audience and build your program from there.

Giving positive reinforcement

Everyone's heard of the ol' carrot-and-stick approach — using a combination of positive (carrot) and negative (stick) reinforcement to guide behavior. Although sticks, such as punishment for an undesired behavior, can be effective (just ask Gordon Ramsey or, for that matter, Joseph Stalin), most people agree that when it comes to motivating people to do what you want them to do, the carrot — usually in the form of recognition or reward — works best.

There's some overlap here with the "recognition" motivator; often, positive reinforcement takes the form of recognizing and thanking people for their good deeds.

The stick in the carrot-and-stick system can be effective. You can punish users who don't behave the way you want them to by, say, deducting points or withdrawing services. But it's best to avoid it. Why? Because it gives customers a negative impression of your brand. Remember: Unless your market is limited to masochists, your goal is to delight people. Taking things away from them is not likely to help you achieve that.

Giving rewards

When law-enforcement agencies seek information about a suspected criminal, they don't offer recognition in return. No, they use perhaps the biggest motivator of all: a reward — typically cold, hard cash. Rewards are valuable to all users.

As you'll discover in Chapter 5, rewards can be tangible (the aforementioned cold, hard cash or, say, free airline tickets or a discount on your next purchase) or virtual (points, badges, levels, and so on).

Maintaining relevance

Nobody wants to look at a bunch of information that has no bearing on their area of interest. People want *relevance*. They don't want to have to sift through pages of content to find what they're looking for. They want the material that satisfies their needs to be right there. And they tend to create and consume content that's relevant to them.

In a gamification program, you want to socialize and share content, products, and processes that are relevant to the user. If a user visits the sports section of a media site, be sure to show rewards that are sports-related (as opposed to a site-wide feed that pulls in content from across the whole site). Make it a point to recognize people's interests. This type of personalization is a huge part of motivating intrinsic behaviors.

Harnessing competition

As mentioned, many people are motivated by an urge to compete. Indeed, competitions — whether for prizes, badges, or honor — are among the oldest forms of recreation. Tapping into this innate desire is a great way to motivate desired user behaviors.

Competition is particularly valuable for engaging top users — the ones who've done everything else there is to do on your site.

Responding to challenges

Users are kept stimulated when new objectives, or challenges, arise. When an experience has multiple game layers, with multiple areas to level up and win, players are motivated to stay engaged. With multiple game layers, users maintain higher levels of interest and involvement.

One gamified environment that works very well for competition is sales applications, in which people track their financial performance relative to that of other colleagues.

Visualizing progress

Anyone who's ever driven cross-country knows the sweet siren song of the map that highlights each major landmark *en route*; looking at it, you can track how far you've come, and just how much farther you have to go. Indeed, with any type of journey — be it a literal one, like the aforementioned coast-to-coast scramble, or a figurative one, such as losing weight — being able to visualize the progress made and distance still to go can be a powerful motivator. Gamification offers a great way to keep users apprised of their progress!

Breaking things down into baby steps

Remember the Bill Murray film *What About Bob?* In the film, Murray plays Bob, a multi-phobic psychiatric patient who wants to follow his psychiatrist (played by the brilliant Richard Dreyfuss) to his vacation home. The problem? Bob's terrified of leaving his house, let alone traveling. To overcome his fears, Bob recites the psychiatrist's mantra: "baby steps." ("Baby steps get on the bus, baby steps down the aisle....")

Everyone knows that baby steps, breaking down larger, overwhelming tasks into smaller, easily accomplished micro-tasks, make it much easier to get things done. Each micro-task becomes a little victory, and the larger task is no longer overwhelming. Using this technique is a great way to motivate users who might otherwise feel overpowered by a task to keep moving forward.

Chapter 3

Object Lesson: Establishing Business Objectives

In This Chapter

▶ Exploring customer-related objectives

▶ Identifying employee-related objectives

▶ Setting benchmarks

*T*empting as it may be to slap a game on your company's Web site and call it a day, gamifying your business is, unfortunately, a bit more compli-cated. The fact is, in order for your gamification efforts to be successful, you must first identify what, exactly, you want to achieve. In other words, you must pinpoint your business objectives.

Every business has a unique set of short-term goals and long-term objectives. For example, maybe you want to increase customer engagement. Perhaps you want to build a community around your Web site. Or maybe you want to improve employee performance. Once you've identified what you want to achieve, you can design a game that helps you achieve it.

In this chapter, you'll see examples of various business objectives and dis-cover the importance of setting benchmarks for meeting those objectives.

For more info about what specific behaviors drive each of these objectives, see Chapter 4.

Broadly speaking, business objectives can be divided into two categories: consumer-related objectives and employee-related objectives. We cover both in this chapter, starting with consumer related objectives.

Public Consumption: Considering Consumer-Related Objectives

Examples of consumer-related objectives include:

- ✔ Fostering engagement
- ✔ Inspiring loyalty and customer retention
- ✔ Increasing conversions
- ✔ Building a community

The examples cited here are by no means an exhaustive list of the consumer-related business objectives you can achieve through gamification. Whatever your objective, odds are that gamification could be employed in some way to help you meet it.

Increasing engagement

In the old days, brands' marketing efforts were decidedly one-way. For example, marketers and advertisers hatched a commercial or a print ad, which consumers watched or looked at. Today, however, the most successful marketing efforts are two-way. That is, consumers actively interact with brands. In this paradigm, engagement — which encompasses all the specific actions and behaviors performed by users on your Web and mobile offerings — is key. It's no wonder engagement — sometimes referred to as *brand interactions* — is business objective *numero uno* for many organizations.

Human Sigma experts John Fleming, PhD, and Jim Asplund contend that engaged customers generate a whopping 1.7 times more revenue than "normal" ones.

Defining engagement

Interestingly, the biggest challenge facing today's companies isn't a lack of apps or social technologies. During the past few years, companies have spent gazillions of dollars on their Web sites, mobile applications, social media tools, and other applications aimed at increasing customer loyalty. The challenge for these companies has been a crippling lack of engagement with these investments. The fact is, customers don't interact with these digital touchpoints in the way companies have intended. They're not *engaged*.

Of course, all this begs the question "What constitutes engagement?" In truth, *engagement* is a sort of catch-all term. At a basic level, engagement centers around getting people to utilize the features of your site or application in the way it was initially intended. Behavior sits at the core of every engagement program. The simplest way to think about behavior is as an action. Common behaviors might include posting, commenting, sharing, writing reviews, or voting.

TIP Ideas like engagement and behavior aren't specific to consumer-centric business objectives. They also pertain to employee-related business objectives. In an employee-facing application, engagement-related behaviors might include answering a question in a knowledge base, sharing information in a wiki, or completing a step in a learning-management system, to name just a few examples. (We talk more about employee-related objectives in the second half of the chapter.)

Measuring engagement: KPIs

Yet another question is, "How does one measure engagement?" That's where things get tricky. Beyond just tracking page views or unique visitors, measuring engagement involves assessing a combination of metrics, also called *key performance indicators* (KPIs). These might include how recently a customer visited your site, how frequently a customer visits your site, how long that customer sticks around per visit, how many behaviors the person performs while on your site, and so on. Which of these metrics is most relevant to you varies depending on your business.

What good is setting a business objective if you have no way of determining whether the objective has been met? Enter key performance indicators (KPIs). Also sometimes referred to as *a key success indicator* (*KSI*), a KPI is a quantifiable measurement used to gauge performance in meeting a goal. After an organization sets a goal, or business objective, it must then establish and track KPIs that relate to that goal. Each KPI is linked to a target value. Using this target value, companies can determine whether the objective has been met.

Setting benchmarks

Part of setting KPIs involves establishing benchmarks — that is, points of reference that you can use to measure progress. Setting benchmarks for a gamification program begins with tracking data beforehand to determine your baseline. This baseline might be the current number of comments received per day, the current number of shares per week, or the current number of registered users. You then decide what numbers you must hit for these behaviors in order for your gamification program to be deemed successful. Then, after your gamification program is up and running, you continue tracking data to see if the numbers change and if your goals are met. We discuss benchmarking in more detail in Chapter 13.

KPIs are the facets of engagement that you choose to track, because they are most relevant to your end goals. With game mechanics, you can boost engagement by increasing user behaviors. That is, you can use gamification to entice users who visit your site to engage in more actions, such as the following:

- Logging in to your site
- Commenting on content or a product
- Sharing something from your site on Facebook or Twitter
- Blogging about your brand
- Writing a review
- Asking a question about a product
- Answering a question about a product
- Bookmarking or curating content
- Watching or sharing a video

Setting your KPIs in turn enables you to increase how often those users visit your site (for example, "lift user frequency") as well as gain valuable insights into your users. Figure 3-1 visualizes a few KPIs that track increasing engagement. You'll learn more about behaviors that can help increase engagement in Chapter 4.

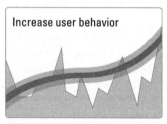

Figure 3-1:
Increasing
engage-
ment.

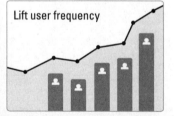

Illustration by Wiley, Composition Services Graphics

Good old loyalty programs

An excellent example of gamification in action, and one you're no doubt already familiar with, is the loyalty program. A *loyalty program* is a structured marketing effort that rewards consumers for purchasing a product or service. Examples of loyalty programs include airline frequent-flyer programs; "buy 10 get one free"–style punch cards at coffee shops, dry cleaners, and similar venues; and so on. In essence, a loyalty program is nothing more than a game in which one is rewarded for winning by achieving status, rewards, and special treatment, be it a free latte or access to a VIP lounge at the airport.

The loyal we: Inspiring loyalty

To some extent, loyalty — in this context, a consumer's affinity for a particular brand and willingness to purchase that brand rather than another — and engagement are interrelated. That is, the more engaged a consumer is with your brand, the more likely that person is to be loyal to it, and vice versa.

Loyalty is particularly critical when products become commoditized. That is, when a competitor's product is nearly indistinguishable from your own in terms of features, price, and availability, it is loyalty that keeps customers in your camp. That said, even for brands that aren't commoditized, engendering loyalty is a critical objective. Indeed, unless the mission of your business parallels that of Dr. Kevorkian's, increased loyalty is a boon for just about any organization.

An important aspect (indeed, some might say the *only* aspect) of loyalty is customer retention — that is, ensuring that your existing customers keep coming back, and often. Successful customer retention starts with the very first "how-dee-do" a company has with a customer and continues throughout the entire lifetime of the relationship. When you consider the costs associated with attracting new customers compared to retaining existing ones — one figure batted around says it takes $10 of new business to replace $1 of lost business — you start to get why retention is so darned important.

Using game mechanics to inspire loyalty can help your business improve its daily return rate, lift the lifetime value of your organization, and increase social referrals (see Figure 3-2).

 With the advent of social media networks such as Facebook and Twitter, word of mouth has become even more powerful due to its increased reach. That makes inspiring loyalty and driving advocacy among customers more important than ever.

Advocadabra: From loyalty to advocacy

The more loyal a person is to your brand, the more likely he or she is to recommend it to others, which is called *brand advocacy*. A person who advocates your brand (a *brand advocate*) doesn't just buy your products, she touts your products to others, including her real-world pals, Facebook friends, Twitter followers, and blog readers. This positive word of mouth is, essentially, free advertising for your brand. Brand advocacy can be quite powerful if the brand advocate has a particularly large personal network. Increasing loyalty, whether through gamification or some other means, may help transform more customers into brand advocates.

Companies are finding that building a platform for fostering and showcasing brand advocacy on their own sites or application is increasingly important. The more you can drive reviews, comments, and other bits of user-generated content that support your products, the more validated people feel prior to purchasing your product or service.

Improve daily return rate

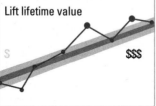

Lift lifetime value

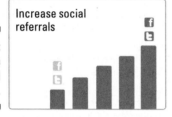

Increase social referrals

Figure 3-2:
The results of increased loyalty.

Illustration by Wiley, Composition Services Graphics

Increasing customer conversion

It's not enough to attract people's interest. As people become more engaged on your site or application, another key business objective is customer conversions. Indeed, if you think about it, engagement, retention, and conversion are linked. Engagement leads to retention, and retention gives you more opportunities for conversion.

Customer conversion involves getting people to perform a set of behaviors that leads to a transaction of some kind. On a retail or e-commerce site, this might include motivating someone to click the Add to Cart button and purchase your product. After all, to sustain your organization, people need to ante up and buy something from you.

One key aspect to converting browsers into buyers is understanding which behaviors users most frequently do before making a purchase. You can find that out by using behavior analytics, which is covered in Chapter 14.

Conversion may mean different things, depending on the life cycle of the product. Early on, it may mean just more exposure — say, getting more registered users or going viral. At some point, though, conversion typically becomes click-throughs and, beyond that, actual product purchases.

Bottom line: Lots of businesses need to convert prospects into customers — and gamification can help you do just that. With game mechanics that emphasize the value of your product, you can obtain more paid conversions, increase user registrations, and accelerate purchase frequency (see Figure 3-3).

Building a community

Many sites seek to build a community — say, an outlet to discuss new products or a place for fans to convene. Despite the proliferation of proprietary online communities, according to Gartner, only 28 percent of customers actually ever log into them, let alone use them in a meaningful way. That's because users often have little reason to return. Just because you put profiles, user generated-content tools, and other social software at users' fingertips on your Web site doesn't mean they'll engage with those elements.

It's a classic chicken-and-egg scenario: If your community is empty, there's no one to post content; and if no one posts content, no one will come visit the community. Enter gamification. With gamification programs, you can reward people for engaging with these communities and encourage them to come back frequently.

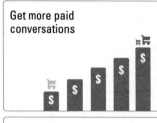

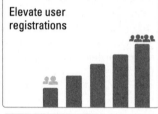

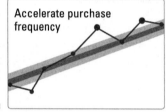

Figure 3-3:
Boosting
conversions
with game
mechanics.

Illustration by Wiley, Composition Services Graphics

One way to reward them is with rank, status, and reputation. For example, if someone goes to an outdoor sporting site and contributes a lot of content about hiking boots, that person could earn points that give him early access to new products. (You'll learn more about rewards in Chapter 5.)

By building a community, you can increase your total number of active users and reduce the *churn*, or attrition, rate. And you'll fain insights about your user distribution (see Figure 3-4).

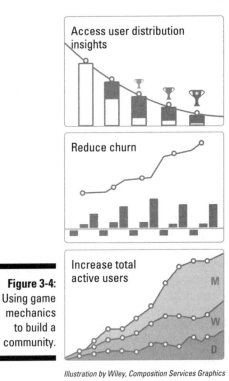

Figure 3-4:
Using game
mechanics
to build a
community.

Illustration by Wiley, Composition Services Graphics

Employee Relations: Exploring Employee-Related Objectives

Examples of employee-related objectives include:

- ✔ Speeding up business processes
- ✔ Enabling sales
- ✔ Encouraging knowledge sharing and collaboration
- ✔ Adoption of new technology
- ✔ Onboarding
- ✔ Improving education and training

Again, that's by no means an exhaustive list of employee-related business objectives that can be achieved through gamification. Whatever your objective, gamification could very well be employed in some degree to help you meet it.

Speeding up business processes

Most business software, though designed to automate business processes, still relies on human participation. For example, companies such as Oracle, Microsoft, Salesforce.com, and others have built sales, financial, and communications technology to make businesses run more efficiently. Quite frequently, though, actual human types must input and manage the data at the proper touchpoints. Often, they don't do so well, resulting in lost productivity and diminishing the value of the extremely expensive software.

For example, consider a support organization in which a key business process is the opening and closing of support tickets in a service desk application. Using gamification, you could recognize key behaviors such as opening a support ticket and closing one. Once the behavior tracking is in place, the system could then reward high-performing employees. In the end, the result would almost certainly be an increase in the rate of closing those tickets (see Figure 3-5).

Figure 3-5:
You can use gamification to reward employees who successfully close tickets in a service desk application like this one.

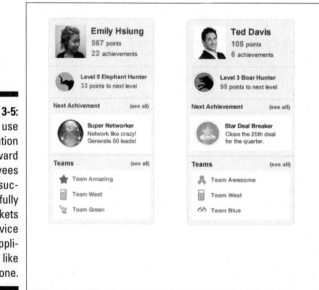

Image courtesy of Badgeville

Sell! Sell! Sell! Enabling sales

Gamification can reward people for performing key business processes in sales applications and, in doing so, speed them up. For example, in a sales application, sales teams must manage their leads and opportunities by inputting critical data points. By measuring and tracking desired behaviors, you can set milestones and showcase success on a leaderboard, as shown in Figure 3-6. The social pressure to succeed can help drive adherence to company processes. They'll naturally fill out more lead forms, creating more opportunities for the business.

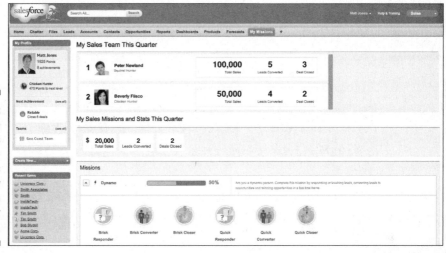

Figure 3-6: Showcasing top sellers on a leaderboard is a great way to motivate your sales staff.

Image courtesy of Badgeville

 In sales, you can also make your game mechanics contextual. So if a salesperson really specializes in selling to the media industry, maybe that person can earn the Media Master achievement for behaviors performed in the application. Figure 3-7 shows examples of contextual rewards (you'll read more about rewards in Chapter 5).

 Gamification is well suited to enabling sales. This is no doubt partly due to the fact that people who work in sales tend to be quite competitive in nature. For more on how gamification can help organizations improve sales, see the appendix at the back of the book.

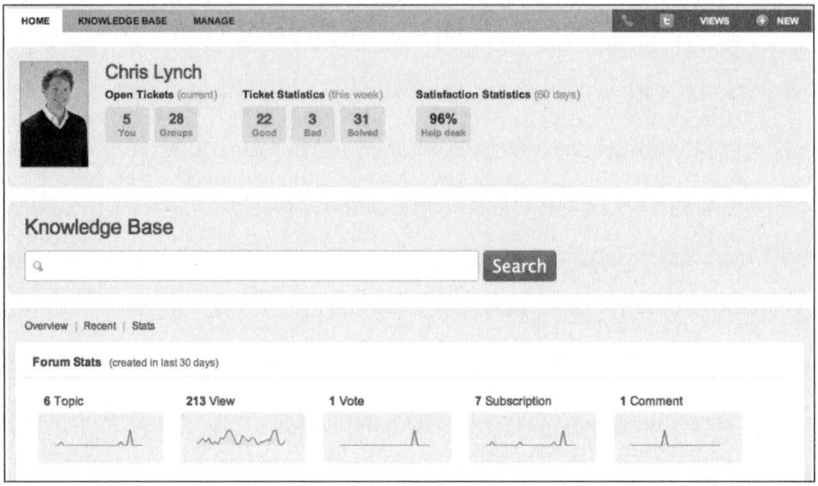

Figure 3-7: Contextual rewards are a great way to recognize employees.

Image courtesy of Badgeville

Knowledge is power: Encouraging knowledge sharing and collaboration

As companies have observed the power of social sites like Facebook, Twitter, and even Wikipedia, they have tried to apply similar principles in their own organizations by providing internal social networks, blogs, wikis, and other technologies to promote knowledge sharing across the workforce. But more often than not, the workforce tends not to use them. According to research from Forrester, a global research and advisory firm, such tools are only adopted by 12 percent of the workforce.

Why not? One reason is that people are resistant to change. They're used to e-mail and their other creature comforts. They also believe knowledge is power, and aren't terribly inclined to surrender that power to others. Using gamification, companies can champion employees who leverage these types of collaborative applications. As people share valuable knowledge, other employees can benefit.

Adoption of new technology

Suppose your company has invested a sum not unlike the gross national product of a small nation on a new database. To make good on that investment, it's imperative that employees use that database — and use it properly. To ensure that happens, you could employ gamification, rewarding employees who adopt the new technology and for continuing to use it correctly.

Aiding with onboarding

These days, to get started at a new company, employees must move through a mountain of digital paperwork. By gamifying certain processes along the way — for example, filling out forms, taking sexual harassment courses, and learning about key company policies — companies can improve the rate at which these tasks are completed.

Improving training and education

At many companies, people must complete various training courses online. The problem is, no one wants to actually complete these courses. In fact, sometimes it seems as if the age-old instinct to play hooky becomes more powerful than ever when you're faced with the prospect of completing online training. By leveraging gamification programs, companies can acknowledge and champion employees who complete important training.

To help in this mission, try leveraging the gentle guide framework (Chapter 9).

Chapter 4

Target Practice: Targeting Desired Behaviors

Chapter 3 identifies several key consumer-related and employee-related business objectives. These range from increasing engagement to speeding up business processes. In this chapter, you'll discover some key behaviors that drive those objectives.

Put simply, behaviors are the foundation of all gamification programs. It's not enough to define your business objectives; you must determine which valuable user behaviors will drive them.

You can determine which game mechanics are most likely to drive those behaviors and reward users for performing them. (You'll explore game mechanics in Chapter 6 and rewards in Chapter 5.)

Just what *is* a behavior? The simplest way to think about a behavior is as a verb — or, to appease you grammarist as out there, a gerund. It's an *ing* word, which is essentially a verb in noun's clothing. Here are a few examples of behaviors:

- ✔ Purchasing
- ✔ Commenting
- ✔ Posting
- ✔ Reviewing
- ✔ Ranking

- ✔ Voting
- ✔ Sharing
- ✔ Collaborating
- ✔ Updating
- ✔ Verifying
- ✔ Checking in

Turning Valued Behaviors into Valuable Behaviors

We like to distinguish between what we call *valued behaviors* and *valuable behaviors*:

- ✔ **Valued behaviors are behaviors that your target audience already performs because those behaviors have an inherent worth to *them*.** For example, on a content site or knowledge base, a valued behavior might be reading or posting content. On an e-commerce site, valued behaviors might include accessing product reviews and purchasing items. Valued behaviors are the innate behaviors people just naturally perform on your site or application.

- ✔ **Valuable behaviors are behaviors that are important to *you*.** They're the ones that drive revenue or growth on your site. They're also the ones that help you meet the business objectives you've identified for your gamification program. So, using the same examples, if you run a content site, valuable behaviors — behaviors in which you would like your users to engage — would likely include writing a blog post or sharing an existing post via Facebook or Twitter. If your site is of the e-commerce variety, then an obvious example of a valuable behavior would be purchasing items. Another valuable behavior might be writing and posting reviews of products purchased.

In a perfect world, your target audience's *valued* behaviors will align perfectly with the behaviors your organization views as *valuable*. That will result in a seamless experience for the user. If they're don't align, your goal is to find a way to make it so they do.

That's where gamification — specifically, rewards — comes in. As you build your program, start by rewarding valued behaviors, the ones users already perform because they're of some worth to the user. Then, as those rewards gain acceptance, slowly layer on rewards for the behaviors you *want* users to perform. If you play your cards right, eventually those *valuable* behaviors will become *valued* behaviors. (As mentioned, we talk about rewards in Chapter 5.)

Unchained melody: Behavior chaining

Sometimes, your focus is on a single behavior. But often, you're after a *series* of behaviors — say, reading content, commenting on content, *and* sharing content. Or maybe it's reading reviews, purchasing the product reviewed, *and then* reviewing the product. This is called *behavior chaining*. Defining behavior chains can yield excellent results.

Sometimes, simply focusing on a threshold behavior — the first behavior in a behavior chain — can prompt the user to automatically complete the rest of the behaviors in the chain. Once you get people to a certain tipping point, the rest comes easy. As an obvious example, if you can persuade someone to jump out of an airplane (the threshold behavior), odds are he'll pull his rip cord to open his parachute with no further prompting from you.

Even if you take this gradual approach, if a behavior you encourage is way out of left field, your users won't bite — unless your reward is crazy compelling. In that case, the user might view the receipt of the reward as being more like a business transaction — in other words, I do this crazy thing for you, and you "pay" me handsomely in return.

Simple Minds: Comparing Simple and Advanced Behaviors

A *simple behavior* is one that doesn't require additional qualifiers to describe. Here are some examples of simple behaviors:

- ✔ Commenting
- ✔ Watching a video
- ✔ Writing a review
- ✔ Responding to a customer inquiry

An *advanced behavior* is a simple behavior with one or more qualifiers. An advanced behavior *qualifier* can be one or more pieces of metadata that narrow the definition of the behavior (see nearby sidebar for more on metadata). For example, based on the aforementioned simple behaviors, advanced behaviors might include the following:

- ✔ Commenting on an article about fashion
- ✔ Watching a video released in the previous week

Tagging metadata

Often, people define the term *metadata* as "data about data." In agamification context, however, a better definition might be "data about content." This type of metadata is often generated through *tagging*. In other words, you tag a behavior with some piece of data — for example,you assign it a time,a category, or what have you.

In the case of our example advanced behaviors, two behaviors involve category tags (the article on which the user comments *must* be about fashion; the review the reader writes *must* be about a specific product), and two involve time tags (the user *must* watch a video released in the previous week; the user *must* respond to a customer inquiry within 30 minutes of receiving it).

  ✔ Writing a review of a specific product

  ✔ Responding to a customer inquiry within 30 minutes of receiving it

When it comes to gamification, the behaviors you motivate can be as simple or as advanced as you want.

Matching Behaviors with Customer-Related Business Objectives

As mentioned, Chapter 3 identified several key consumer-related business objectives. To review, these were as follows:

  ✔ Fostering engagement

  ✔ Inspiring loyalty

  ✔ Increasing conversions

  ✔ Building a community

In this section, you'll discover some specific behaviors that can help drive each of those business objectives, as well as the key performance indicators (KPIs) involved.

Behaviors that foster engagement

Fostering engagementencompasses all the specific actions and behaviors performed by users on your Web and mobile offerings. Fostering engagement is objective *numero uno* for many businesses. Not surprisingly, it's also one of the most difficult objectives to meet.

In many respects, the behaviors that pertain to engagement depend on what type of site you run. For example, on a content site, content is key; so the behaviors that drive engagement — and therefore the behaviors you will want to reward — relate to the generation of content and, to a lesser extent, the consumption of content. These behaviors include the following:

- ✔ Posting a comment
- ✔ Writing a blog post
- ✔ Reading existing content
- ✔ Voting on content
- ✔ Rating content

Continuing with the content-site example, consider that roughly 90 percent of users on this type of site are *lurkers*, who consume but don't contribute. Typically, 9 percent of users are casually involved, and the remaining 1 percent are your power users. To keep all these users involved, you want to reward all these different types of behavior. And to do that, you first have to measure them.

The key performance indicators (KPIs) associated with those behaviors might include the following:

- ✔ Number of comments
- ✔ Number of blog posts
- ✔ Number of page views
- ✔ Number of votes
- ✔ Number of ratings entered

"Gee," you're thinking. "That's all really interesting. But my site *isn't* a content-related site. What behaviors do *I* need to focus on in order to drive engagement?" Glad you asked — although you may not be thrilled with our answer, which is, "It depends," and further, "You'll kind of have to figure that out yourself."

Our advice? Start by examining the common valued behaviors on your site — the behaviors in which your users naturally engage — and work from there. Recognizing them for things they're already doing is a great way to motivate them to do more.

Ask: "How do my users spend time on my site, and how can I measure this in a meaningful way?"

One way to identify this is through behavior tracking. That is, before you add a gamified element to your site, measure what behaviors your top users already perform. Once you have that baseline in place, you might be able to glean some idea about what behaviors you want to track more of. For example, on a health Web site, a key behavior might be logging workout minutes.

If you think of engagement as measurable activity, and if you want to increase measurable activity, one answer is to recognize as many different useful behaviors as you can.

Behaviors that inspire loyalty

Loyalty is a consumer's affinity for a particular brand and willingness to purchase that brand rather than another. Loyalty and engagement are interrelated. That is, the more engaged a consumer is with your brand, the more likely that person is to be loyal to it (and vice versa). As a result, you can reasonably assume that many of the behaviors that foster engagement will also inspire loyalty.

That being said, inspiring loyalty *is* different from fostering engagement. One way to inspire loyalty is to use rewards to instill a sense of progress in the user — for example, buy two doohickeys, get the third doohickey for free. Or buy five doohickeys and receive free shipping for life. The behavior you're focusing on is, obviously, purchasing.

You can also recognize users for simply patronizing the site. If you do a great job of making a user feel welcome, but your competition treats the user like a nobody, then that user will naturally begin to feel more loyal to your site. And of course, you should make a special effort to recognize users who advocate for your brand; such recognition can serve to deepen their loyalty. Everybody likes to feel like they're somebody.

The KPIs associated with purchasing and patronizing might include the following:

 ✔ Number of purchases
 ✔ Number of logins

Using metadata can help foster loyalty because it allows you to get more granular and contextual in the behaviors that matter to your users. For example, if you know that someone visiting an electronics Web site writes a lot of reviews about mobile phones, you can probably assume she will enjoy receiving a Mobile Master badge and appearing on a mobile-specific leaderboard.

Behaviors that increase conversions

Of course, a key part of increasing conversions — getting people to a transaction of some kind — is boosting engagement and loyalty. After all, to sustain your organization, people need to ante up and buy something from you. But often, increasing conversions involves more than that. Specifically, it involves *proving value.*

When you're talking about conversions, you're generally not talking about people who already use your product or site. You're talking about new users being introduced to your product or site. So the really important thing here is showing them all the key features of your product or site, showing them that other users are present, as well as showing how other users who login with the site are being rewarded for their participation. In some ways, the behaviors you want to reward, then, pertain to learning. Your goal is to teach the user what the site or product is or does.

We assume your product is valuable. If it's crap, you're not going to be able to use gamification to convince the user that it's good.

Consider a health and fitness site where your goal is to convert a trial member to a full subscriber. To "prove" the worth of the site, you might prompt users to engage in these learning behaviors:

- ✔ Exploring various program offerings
- ✔ Visiting other users' pages
- ✔ Reading reviews of the site

The KPIs associated with those behaviors might include:

- ✔ Number of page views of program offering pages
- ✔ Number of page views of other users' pages
- ✔ Number of page views of review pages

Once the user has decided to convert, you might switch to rewarding the behaviors on which the site itself is centered:

- ✔ Choosing a program
- ✔ Logging physical activity
- ✔ Logging results
- ✔ Sharing results

Behaviors that build community

As you know, the goal of many sites is to build a community. But as mentioned in Chapter 3, according to Gartner, only 28 percent of customers actually engage with these communities. It's not enough to make profiles, user generated-content tools, and other social software available to users. You have to give them a super-compelling reason to use them.

The key to promoting community-building behaviors is realizing that the required behaviors are social in nature. These include the following:

- ✔ Leaving comments
- ✔ Writing reviews
- ✔ Giving a "thumbs up" or "high five" (or whatever they're called on your site)
- ✔ Asking a question
- ✔ Answering a question
- ✔ Sharing an idea

Sharing ideas is often called ideation. Creative in nature, *ideation* can be thought of as the process of generating, developing, and communicating new ideas. It occurs in all stages of a thought cycle and is an essential part of the design process. No wonder it's considered a high-value behavior.

The KPIs associated with the aforementioned behaviors might include the following:

- ✔ Number of comments
- ✔ Number of reviews
- ✔ Number of "thumbs ups" or "high fives"
- ✔ Number of questions asked
- ✔ Number of questions answered
- ✔ Number of ideas shared

Be aware that for each community, the most valuable behaviors you want to drive may vary. For example, in a support community, you might reward people for being the first to reply to a question about a product. In a health and fitness community, you might recognize people for sharing their progress with the group. Note that as people engage with your community, their rank and status should be elevated as well.

You need to really know your community before selecting the behaviors you want to reward. For example, rewarding competitive behaviors in a community that's more cooperative will almost certainly end in heartbreak and recriminations — or, more specifically, disgust, anger, disinterest, and departure.

Aligning Behaviors with Employee-Related Business Objectives

In addition to identifying key consumer-related business objectives, Chapter 3 also pinpoints some critical employee-related business objectives. To refresh your memory, these were as follows:

- ✔ Speeding up business processes
- ✔ Enabling sales
- ✔ Encouraging knowledge sharing and collaboration
- ✔ Aiding with onboarding
- ✔ Improving training and education

In this section, you'll discover some specific behaviors that can help drive each of those business objectives.

Behaviors that speed up business processes

Every business has *processes* — activities or sets of activities designed to accomplish a specific goal. Although businesses invest loads of dough in software to automate these processes, actual people must input and manage the data involved — except when they don't, which, it turns out, is often. The result? A slowing of business processes and a general loss in productivity — not to mention that there's no return on that huge investment you made.

To turn that around, you can emphasize various behaviors among your employees; the specific behaviors will vary depending on the scenario. For example, say you run a service department that responds to customer complaints. The key behaviors associated with speeding up business processes might include the following:

✔ Responding to an issue

✔ Resolving the issue

✔ Updating records associated with the issue

For even better results, you could upgrade these behaviors from simple ones to complex ones by being more specific, with time as your qualifier:

✔ Responding to an issue within 30 minutes

✔ Resolving the issue within 24 hours

✔ Updating records associated with the issue within three days

The KPIs associated with the aforementioned behaviors might include the following:

✔ Total number of complaints addressed

✔ Total number of complaints resolved

✔ Duration of each open complaint

✔ Percentage of complaints resolved

✔ Number of records updated

✔ Percentage of relevant records updated

✔ Duration between resolution of complaint and updating of record

Gamifying these behaviors — or, really, just about any behaviors — can be even more effective if you make the results visible to other employees in the company. When everyone across the company can see who is being rewarded for a behavior, more employees tend to adopt the behavior. This is thanks to a little thing middle-school counselors call "peer pressure."

Behaviors that enable sales

You can use gamification to reward people in sales for performing key behaviors. In sales, these key behaviors include the following:

✔ Calling, emailing, or meeting with a customer

✔ Responding to a lead

✔ Following up on a lead

✔ Converting a lead into an opportunity

✔ Closing a deal (with extra credit for larger deals)

As with speeding up business processes, you might see even better results by upgrading some of these behaviors from simple ones to complex ones — again, with time as your qualifier:

- ✔ Responding to a lead within 30 minutes
- ✔ Following up on a lead within three days
- ✔ Converting a lead to an opportunity within three weeks

Upgrading to this kind of complexity enables you to both recognize people who meet their lead response quota as well as those who are doing it in a timely manner.

The KPIs associated with the aforementioned behaviors might include the following:

- ✔ Number of customer interactions
- ✔ Number of leads received
- ✔ Duration between receipt of lead and pursuit of lead
- ✔ Number of leads pursued
- ✔ Number of leads converted to opportunities
- ✔ Percentage of leads converted to opportunities
- ✔ Number of deals closed

Behaviors that encourage knowledge sharing and collaboration

So your company has invested a boatload in tools to help employees share knowledge and collaborate. The problem? Nobody's using the tools. As mentioned in Chapter 3, this might be because people are resistant to change, preferring e-mail and their other creature comforts. It could also be that they believe knowledge is power — and would prefer to keep that power to themselves. With gamification, companies can recognize employees who leverage collaborative applications.

Improving knowledge sharing and collaboration can also speed up productivity — another common business objective.

To drive knowledge sharing and collaboration, companies could reward behaviors such as the following:

✔ Asking questions

✔ Answering questions

✔ Voting on answers

✔ Receiving votes for your answers

✔ Checking in at customer meetings

Why reward people for checking in at customer meetings? Simple. Because when they check in, you can prompt them to enter additional information, such as the subject of the meeting or the industry to which it pertains. For example, suppose an employee checks in for a meeting with a beverage distributor. If that employee checks in multiple times with the same sector, then other employees will start to recognize that person as having some knowledge in that sector — especially if you award him a Beverage Expert badge that's visible to everyone in the community. Then, if someone else in the company — say, at a different location — has a business opportunity in that sector, she'll know whom to ask for help.

The KPIs associated with the aforementioned behaviors might include the following:

✔ Number of questions asked

✔ Number of questions answered

✔ Number of votes received

✔ Number of check-ins

Behaviors that help with onboarding

Gamifying the onboarding process — that looming mountain of digital paperwork faced by all new employees at a company — can help companies improve the rate at which these tasks are completed. To improve onboarding, consider gamifying the following behaviors:

✔ Reading about company policies

✔ Completing compliance training

✔ Filling out HR forms

✔ Setting up health insurance, 401k, and retirement benefits

The KPIs associated with the aforementioned behaviors might include the following:

- Number of page views for company policies
- Number of compliance training modules completed
- Number of questions answered
- Number of completed HR forms received
- Number of benefit forms received

Behaviors that improve education and training

Many companies ask their employees to complete various training courses online — which, naturally, the employees would prefer not to do. Fortunately, you can take steps to gamify the experience by rewarding certain behaviors, such as the following:

- Starting a training course
- Advancing to the next module of the course
- Answering questions correctly
- Completing the course

Arguably, that last behavior — completing the course — is the most important one. For that, you could offer an extra special reward or broadcast that the user has earned some type of certification. By leveraging gamification programs, companies can acknowledge and champion employees who complete training.

The KPIs associated with the aforementioned behaviors might include the following:

- Number of training courses started
- Number of modules completed
- Number of questions answered correctly
- Number of questions answered incorrectly
- Percentage of questions answered correctly
- Number of courses completed
- Percentages of courses completed

Bad Dog! Identifying Behaviors You Want to Discourage

Just as you should identify behaviors you want to encourage, you should also identify those that you want to discourage. Apart from your garden-variety bad behaviors (sloth, wrath, and so on), you must be aware of exploitative behaviors — behaviors devised by users to game your system.

For example, suppose every user who earns 10,000 points on your site wins a free coffee mug. Suppose further that users receive 100 points for each comment on the site. Cheaters might attempt to game your system by entering dozens of nonsense comments at a time. They're not really doing what you want them to do — they're probably not reading the content on your site, and they're certainly not providing a thoughtful response to it. They're just tapping keys on a keyboard to accumulate points.

Fortunately, there are steps you can take to minimize these types of behaviors. In this case, you might decide to reward users not for entering comments, but instead reward them when others give their comment a "thumb's up." You'll find out more about combating undesirable behaviors in Chapter 6.

Chapter 5

You Win! The Rewards of Rewarding

In This Chapter

▶ Identifying types of rewards

▶ Exploring the use of badges

▶ Choosing rewards

▶ Deciding when to give rewards

*O*dds are, your local bowling alley, shopping mall, or supermarket features what we like to call the Claw of Death, so named because it's a game that's nearly impossible to win. If you're not familiar with it, the Claw of Death — also called a Teddy Picker, Candy Crane, Grab Machine, and Claw Crane — features (wait for it) a claw, which the player manipulates using a joystick in an attempt to grab any one of a variety of prizes, such as plush toys, jewelry, hats, balls, dolls, shirts, candy, and so on. Usually, in order to "win" (that is, to successfully retrieve one of the prizes), the player must make several attempts — this, despite the fact that the prize is inevitably of poor quality and will almost certainly be discarded in the near future.

The Claw of Death stands as a powerful testament to the power of rewards: Even the mere *hope* of receiving a reward — even a really lousy one — can motivate a player to perform a desired behavior. Given this, it makes sense that successful gamification hinges on the use of rewards (preferably good ones). This chapter explores the types of rewards available to you and how best to issue them.

Types of Rewards

As mentioned, the Claw of Death offers a variety of prizes, or rewards, to entice people to play. Similarly, you can attract users to your gamified site using various types of rewards. Your rewards, however, probably won't be a lousy knock-off cartoon plush (unless your users are into that kind of thing).

Arguably, rewards can be divided into three categories:

- ✔ Recognition
- ✔ Privileges
- ✔ Monetary rewards

Conferring recognition

As mentioned in Chapter 2, pretty much everyone wants to be recognized for their achievements. Indeed, recognition is part of just about every type of competition on this (or, presumably, any other) planet. Recognition for completing a task or accomplishing a goal not only feeds this basic human need, it also encourages engagement and increases repetition — both of which are probably in your list of business objectives.

In a gamified system, you can recognize your users in a couple different ways:

- ✔ Reputation
- ✔ Status

Rewarding with reputation

For some users, it's all about reputation. They want to be *respected*. Maybe one of your users is a highly regarded string theorist. Or maybe one of your users knows everything there is to know about, say, string cheese.

Regardless of the subject, rewarding these users for their expertise is key — assuming, of course, that their expertise relates to your area of business. That is, if you run a site about string theory, then rewarding the string-cheese expert probably wouldn't make much sense. By rewarding them for expertise, you enable a user to develop a reputation on your site. This serves two purposes: It demonstrates to others who on the site really knows their stuff, and it enriches the experience of those users who develop a strong reputation on the site. This, in turn, increases the likelihood that he or she will continue to patronize the site.

A good reputation can elevate your status in a community — which can lead to a new job or other opportunities. So although reputation itself isn't a monetary reward, it could *lead* to a monetary reward in the form of a higher salary.

The recognition of expertise or knowledge within a community is a critical element of any gamification program — and a natural byproduct of it. As you earn rewards, it automatically informs your reputation across the site.

Reputation mechanics

Ideally, your gamification efforts will involve the application of *reputation mechanics*, which enable a company's customers, employees, and partners to carry their reputation with them across a company's various sites and applications. For example, if a help desk employee attains a certain reputation in the company's internal support application based on valuable behaviors she performs, that person should be able to carry that reputation with her when she engages in an external support community with customers. As customers, partners, and employees perform valuable behaviors, reputation mechanics allow companies to boost users' rank and status across all their sites and applications.

With internal business environments, reputation can be tied to specific expertise — a very powerful feature. That's because on most of today's social networks, reputation is stated instead of earned. If you fill out your social networking profile and make yourself a self-proclaimed "expert" in support, that's not as powerful as being an expert based on your valuable behaviors and associated rewards that make you, say, a Level 5 Support Expert. Simply put, reputation in a gamification program is based not on what you *say* you're good at doing, but on what you *do*.

Another great thing about reputation is it brings credibility to a gamified environment. Any jerk can leave a comment, but in a gamified system that emphasizes reputation, other users can assess how useful that comment is. So on the one hand, reputation is a reward; but on the other, it brings contextual meaning to a gamification program.

Rewarding with status

Chapter 2 makes a big deal about status. Whereas reputation is tied to expertise and a body of work, status refers to the relative position of one individual compared to another, with those having a higher position or rank being conferred greater status. And no wonder! Anyone who's ever walked down Rodeo Drive in Beverly Hills, with all the crazy-expensive clothes, cars, and whatnot on display, knows how critical status is to people. Especially in a social environment, people are very concerned with status.

As you find out in Chapter 6, you can use various game mechanics, such as points, leaderboards, and levels, to denote status as well as reputation.

In a gamified environment, status is often tied to valuable behaviors that support a company's business objectives. So on a site that sells books, for example, you might reward users who submit particularly excellent reviews. If your goal is to foster engagement on, say, a weight-loss site, then you could confer higher status on those users who religiously add entries to their online food journals.

You can confer status (and, for that matter, reputation) using the following tools:

✔ **Badges:** Ever been a Boy Scout or a Girl Scout? Then you're already familiar with the idea behind badges, such as the Stamp Collecting, Bugling, and ever-useful Nuclear Science merit badges available to Boy Scouts and Girl Scouts nationwide. To quote Merriam-Webster, a *badge* is "an emblem awarded for a particular accomplishment." Badges, which can serve both to incite a player to action and to reward the player for completing a task, can be either physical (like the aforementioned Boy Scout merit badges, which are sewn onto one's Boy Scout uniform) or virtual (like the badges one earns on various Web sites; see Figure 5-1). The latter is more common in gamification programs. Badges are kind of a *big deal*. Which is why there's a whole section devoted to them later in this chapter. Read on!

Figure 5-1:
Virtual
badges are
common in
gamification
programs.

Image courtesy of Zurmo

✔ **Levels:** Levels represent status in your gamification program. Players advance to new levels by performing behaviors and earning points. (More on points in the next chapter.) It's a good idea to make the first few levels easier to attain because that encourages users to participate more often. The highest levels may require extended usage over a longer period. (See Figure 5-2.)

✔ **Leaderboards:** A leaderboard is a board that displays the names and scores of current competitors in a gamified system. Alternatively, a leaderboard might simply indicate a player's ranking in the system without noting the scores of others (see Figure 5-3). Levels and leaderboards are both ways to indicate a player's status or reputation. A user who reaches a certain level on a site or attains a high position on the site's leaderboard will naturally be recognized as being of a higher status than users who have not yet attained that level or position.

Figure 5-2:
Levels are
sometimes
indicated
by trophy
icons. Based
on your
audience
preferences,
you might
decide to
define any-
where from
two levels
(say, rookie
and veteran)
to hundreds,
but most
sites have
somewhere
between five
and ten.

Image courtesy of Badgeville

Figure 5-3:
An example
of a leader-
board.

Image courtesy of Zurmo

Badges, levels, and leaderboards are most effective when employed on a social site. Without that social component (see Figure 5-4), you'll find that these types of rewards simply aren't as useful. For many, status just isn't all that meaningful if no one else knows about it.

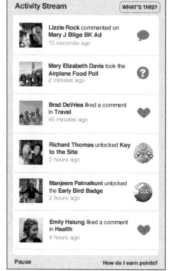

Figure 5-4:
Status
is more
important on
social sites
with activity
streams like
this one.

Image courtesy of Badgeville

Social mechanics

For many, status just isn't that meaningful if nobody knows you have it. That's where social mechanics come in. *Social mechanics* leverage the same dynamics that power social networks like Facebook, Twitter, and LinkedIn by applying them to the websites and applications of world-class companies. By connecting users with relevant people and the valuable behaviors they perform, social mechanics help companies drive meaningful engagement with their products, content, and services.

Often, social mechanics take the form of an activity stream on a site or app that notifies users about relevant behaviors their peers are performing in real time (Figure 5-4). This encourages and motivates those users to engage and follow in their peers' footsteps. For example, if you're on a website and you notice in the activity stream that someone you know read an article on that site, you might be more inclined to read that article yourself. In a way, the social reinforcement users derive from social mechanics becomes a reward in and of itself.

Giving privileges

Although some users prefer to be rewarded with reputation or status, others will be more motivated by receiving privileges. These might include the following:

- Early/VIP access
- Moderation powers
- Stronger votes

Early/VIP access

Suppose your site is of the e-commerce variety, and every so often you have sales — big ones, involving giant discounts. What if you were to reward your top customers with the privilege of accessing those sales early — say, with a 30-minute head start? Think about it: Giving your best customers dibs on sale items not only makes them feel important, it increases the likelihood that they'll buy from you again. At the same time, it doesn't have the same costly effect on your bottom line has giving stuff away for free or at aggressively discounted prices.

Other examples of access-based rewards include the following:

- Early access to new products
- Access to premium content
- VIP seating
- Earlier appointments for services needed
- Access to key personnel in your company (say, lunch with the chairman of the board)

Moderation powers

One way to reward users is to empower them. For example, on a forum site, you might endow your top thread starters with the power to moderate the site. This is doubly excellent, because the user is typically thrilled to take on this responsibility, and you essentially receive free labor.

Giving users powers over the general riff-raff is also a way of conferring status.

Stronger votes

To quote George Orwell: "All animals are equal, but some animals are more equal than others." Which is why you might decide to give some of your users stronger votes — on a site in which content is voted up or down, for example, or on a site that involves rating products.

Giving monetary rewards

Some users will certainly be satisfied with recognition and privileges, but others may hold out for more tangible benefits. These benefits are typically monetary in nature, but could also involve free stuff. Here are a few examples of monetary rewards:

- ✔ Discounts
- ✔ Free shipping
- ✔ Prizes
- ✔ Redemptions

The use of monetary rewards for a gamification program should be considered carefully. Why? Read on to find out.

Mo' money, mo' problems: MIT on monetary rewards

In a recent MIT study, people were promised monetary rewards, tied to their level of performance. If the tasks were thoughtless and menial, higher overall rewards encouraged higher performance. If, however, the tasks required creative problem-solving, higher rewards caused poorer performance. There are a few possible explanations for these results:

- ✔ Rewards increased the stakes, causing stress.

- ✔ Rewards belittled the task by applying a value to it. (For example, with no rewards, the subject is doing the experimenter a favor, which he feels good about; with a $5 reward, the subject is being paid a measly $5 for his labor.)

- ✔ The difference in value between the top reward and the "mediocre" reward wasn't enough to encourage increased performance. Poor performance was also rewarded, just not as much.

- ✔ Monetary rewards are extrinsic motivators and are therefore less motivating than intrinsic motivators. (For more on extrinsic and intrinsic motivators, flip back to Chapter 2.)

Our suspicion? Some combination of all of the above was at play during the MIT experiments. Regardless, you'll likely achieve best results if you reserve monetary rewards for situations where status and reputation don't apply: either solo experiences where there aren't other players to appreciate status, or for top users who already have all the reputation they can get.

Discounts

You can reward top customers with special discounts on your products. Or, you might offer customers a one-time discount if they perform a desired behavior — say, registering with the site or tweeting about your business.

Free shipping

If you've ever shopped at Amazon.com, you're probably familiar with this reward: The site offers free shipping as a reward to users who spend at least $25 on eligible products. Similarly, some businesses offer free shipping to their top customers as a way of saying thanks.

Prizes

Perhaps the most obvious example of the use of prizes is McDonald's Monopoly, based on the famous Hasbro board game of the same name. In this game, which the company has run every year since 1987, McDonald's customers receive a game piece with the purchase of select menu items. Some of these pieces are of the "instant win" variety, typically for a menu item such as French fries or a drink. Other game pieces correspond to a property space on a Monopoly board; by collecting them, players can win additional, awesomer prizes. An online counterpart, introduced in 2005, enables players to participate further by entering codes to roll a pair of virtual dice and move around an online Monopoly board.

Why has McDonald's Monopoly been such a successful rewards play? Because customers quickly realize that if they do something, they get something — with a chance to win even more. That is, no matter what, you're probably going to win some fries or a Coke, and you *might* win something big, like a vacation or a car or some significant Benjamins. And with the online component, you could argue the promotion is even more successful; customers are incited to perform a valuable advanced behavior (that is, go to McDonald's, purchase a select menu item, or visit the McDonald's Monopoly website).

As evidenced by the McDonald's Monopoly example, prizes can be literally anything, small or large, from a wee food item to a gigantor cash jackpot. But the easiest type of prize to give is whatever you have on hand — fries or a soda. Are you an electronics retailer? Then electronics are the logical choice as prizes. Do you sell clothing? Then it makes sense to reward users with duds. Another good type of prize is one that broadcasts your brand — say, a coffee mug or baseball cap with your logo.

Although prizes generate buzz and excitement, offering them is expensive and may not result in lasting engagement or even positive feelings on the part of users. This is especially true if the prize is stuff rather than an experience. That is, if someone wins a TV, that TV will likely decrease in value (emotionally speaking) over time. In contrast, if someone wins a trip to Italy, the trip will increase in value due to the happy memories that result.

Sometimes, monetary rewards can pollute the equation. This is particularly true for altruistic sites. Why? Because it can make people feel less charitable — which is a problem if your site centers around encouraging people to give.

Redemptions

Many companies opt to reward desired behaviors with points — sometimes called something else, such as *miles* — that users can redeem for, well, just about anything. Take American Express, for example. It enables cardmembers to earn points for each dollar spent, which they can redeem for goods ranging from gift cards for retail stores and restaurants to convert tickets, airline tickets, and more. Cardmembers can even redeem points to donate to any of more than a million charities.

Typically, consumers expect to receive one point for each dollar spent. When they go to redeem them, they generally assume they'll get $1 (or equivalent goods) for every 100 points earned.

To make sure no one accrues, like, a *billion* points over their lifetime, and then cashes them out all at once (thereby bankrupting your organization), you might set things up so that any points a person earns expire at some point — say, after two years.

In addition to redeeming points for goods, many companies also enable consumers to redeem points for cash. Discover is an excellent example of this, offering cash back — anywhere from 2–5%, depending on the type of card and the purchase made.

If you're a larger company with an existing loyalty program, you may need to decide how to align gamification-based points with your traditional loyalty points. In some cases, you may integrate them. In other cases, you'll need to keep them separate.

You'll read more about points, including redeemable points, in Chapter 6.

Badges? We don't need no stinking badges! Actually, maybe you do

The Mexican bandits in *Treasure of the Sierra Madre* may not have needed badges, but odds are your gamification program does. As mentioned, badges are emblems awarded for a particular accomplishment — or, in gamification-ese, for the performance of a particular behavior, such as learning a new skill. Badges are so important in gamification that they merit a section all their own.

Badges are visual proof that a user has completed a specific task or unlocked certain privileges, marking the completion of goals within the gamified environment. Badges both reward player action and — assuming the badges are visible to others on the site (hint: They totally should be) — confer status, making them a powerful motivator.

Badges are often used as status items. As such, they must be visible to other users. If they're not, their meaning and value is limited.

If you think about it, the act of leveling up to get a badge has been around forever. You've no doubt experienced it yourself, playing common arcade games. Take Ms. PacMan, released in 1981. As you probably know, the premise is pretty simple: You cruise around a maze eating dots and try to avoid being eaten by ghosts. Unlike its ancestor, PacMan, Ms. PacMan has levels, each one featuring a different food (mostly fruits, but also a pretzel). Essentially, each of these foods — which appears along the bottom of the screen when you "eat" it — is a badge.

The idea of leveling up and getting a badge isn't limited to games; it's present in many other parts of life. We mentioned scouting, but what about the military? Same deal. You do things, you level up, you get badges (stripes and medals, for example). The longer you serve, the more you do, the higher levels you reach in terms of levels, status, and recognition. There are loads of rewards that can be "unlocked" (see Figure 5-5).

Figure 5-5:
Military medals are great examples of real-world badges.

Photo by Danielle Keller, used under Creative Commons License

Badges also speak to some people's innate desire to collect things (as evidenced by your dearly departed great-aunt's collection of useless decorative porcelain doodads). A collection of badges can signify the experiences some-one has had and the achievements earned along the way. On a consumer site, this might involve collecting badges based on ratings, reviews, and posts about specific products. Inside a company, users can collect badges related to key milestones pertaining to their job.

Badges even factor into education: Do things (take tests, write papers), level up (go from grade to grade), get a badge (gold star, A+, PhD). Indeed, this simple concept — do things, level up, get a badge — is a foundation for moti-vation and human behavior. Do things at work (convert a lead to a sale), level up (receive a promotion), get a badge (window office, nicer car).

Naming badges

The name you give a badge should be meaningful, both to the person who receives the badge and to others who are able to view it. In general, the key to naming a badge is to keep it contextually relevant to the user. If it's a customer-facing Web site, work with some of the naming conventions you already have in place for sections of the site or specific products. If it's an employee-facing application, try to tie badges to something meaningful within a job function or department.

For example, a Commenter badge might only have limited meaning to a baseball fan who visits a sports site. But the Harry Caray badge, named after the famous Chicago Cubs commentator, will almost certainly be more significant to them.

Table 5-1 shows an example of an effective badge system, with powerful names. Notice how it enables users to easily earn the first two badges and becomes progressively more challenging from there. This is a key aspect of designing an effective rewards system. (More on this later in this chapter.)

Table 5-1	An Effective Badge System	
Badge	*Activity*	*Purpose*
Noob	Create an account	This badge is for new users, to welcome them to the site.
Opinionator	Post10 comments	This award is for users who are just beginning to participate on the site.
Conversationalist	Start 5 new threads	This award is for users who start new conversations, also called *threads.*
Scintillator	Receive 20 comments	This is for users who start a par-ticularly riveting conversation.

Designing badges

Visually, badges should be eye-catching works of art. Think about it: A badge is just one wee piece of crowded screen real estate. It should stand out. Badges represent effort and accomplishment; as such, your goal is to design badges that users will value.

Beyond that, you should be aware of several practical considerations when designing effective rewards. Here are a few:

- ✔ Theme
- ✔ Iconography
- ✔ Shape
- ✔ Groups

Theme

Badges should be thematically relevant to your site. For example, a site with a pirate theme might use treasure as the basis for badges. The first time someone visits the site, he might receive a bronze coin badge; the 50th time he logs in, he might earn a badge festooned with a jeweled crown. Or maybe your site pertains to birds; in that case, you could develop a series of badges that depict different types of tweeters (see Figure 5-6).

Figure 5-6:
How cute
are these
badges?
Aren't you
dying to
earn one?

Image courtesy of MNN.com

Although employing a theme is not strictly required, doing so will help you design a program that feels cohesive and purposeful.

Iconography

A common error for people new to badge design is to create intricate badges that are rich with detail. While those types of badges may seem very appealing when viewed on a large screen, details — including text — will likely be lost when the image is reduced to actual size. Badges are small.

When designing badges, consider these important tips:

✔ Review the image in its intended size to confirm that the design works as a badge.

✔ If you incorporate text, make sure you can read it when the badge is displayed.

✔ Supported file types depend on your gamification platform, but recommend formats include PNG (recommended), JPEG, and GIF.

✔ Color bit depth should be 32 bits or less.

✔ The recommended size is 64×64 pixels, but up to 80×80 is also okay.

Shape

Many sites employ badges that are simply circular in shape. But if a different, more interesting shape will appeal to your audience, opt for that instead. You can use the shape of a badge to codify different types or levels of badges. (See Figure 5-7.)

Figure 5-7: Although circular badges are popular, badges can be any shape.

Image courtesy of Badgeville

Groups

A badge can be a singleton or part of a group of two or more badges that are part of a mission (see Chapter 6 for more on missions). Most missions use two group types: progressions and collections.

A *progression group*, also called a ladder, is used to reward a user for performing a specific behavior more frequently (one, five, 10^5, or however many times). Visiting, commenting, sharing an article, and viewing a video are all behaviors that could be implemented as a progression or ladder. Badges in a progression should show progression in a visual manner with appropriate use of color, number, and/or complexity.

Here are a few tips to keep in mind with respect to progression groups:

✔ Color progression could be dark to bright hues of the same color, or vice versa.

✔ Avoid using numeric values unless the image alone fails to convey the desired message.

✔ If you decide to use numbers as a means of depicting frequency of behavior (see Figure 5-8), then use numbers for all progressive collections — across all behaviors that are progressively rewarded like visiting, commenting, reading articles, and so on.

Figure 5-8:
You can use numbers as a way to depict frequency of behavior; otherwise, the use of numbers is best avoided.

Image courtesy of Badgeville

✔ One way to convey progression is to move from a simple design to a more complex design. This complexity can be depicted in many ways. For example, you could tell a story like the one in Figure 5-9, where with every visit, you see the robot coming together with additional parts. Increasing complexity could also be depicted with more contrasting starbursts, as shown in Figure 5-10.

Figure 5-9:
You're not just performing behaviors . . . you're *building a robot*!

Image courtesy of Badgeville

Image courtesy of Badgeville

With every new badge, the visual appeal should be enhanced. Users should want to progress further and earn more badges in that collection.

In contrast, a *collection* is a group of rewards that does not communicate progression. You use collections to group rewards that are related but not sequential, such as visiting all areas of your site or playing a scavenger hunt. Figure 5-11 shows a collection of badges earned for reading articles in different locations on a travel site; Figure 5-12 features a collection of badges available to people for viewing clips on a video site.

Figure 5-11:
A collection
of badges.

Image courtesy of Badgeville

How do you know when you're finished designing a badge? A good test would be to ask to someone who hasn't seen your badges before to see the art for each badge and guess what behavior it is meant to reward.

What is the meaning of this? Charging rewards with meaning

Suppose you performed some heroic deed. Maybe you tackled some hooligan as he made off with your elderly neighbor's handbag. Or you rescued a kitten from a tree. Suppose further that to recognize you, the mayor of your town sent you a letter. Only, the letter was clearly a form letter, with an electronic signature at the bottom. It'd probably be pretty meaningless, huh?

That's the trick to rewarding: filling your rewards with meaning. You can't just develop a bunch of generic rewards, sit back, and watch the magic happen. Sure, that might give you a short-term lift, but if you want your gamification efforts to be successful, you must offer rewards that *mean* something.

This is particularly true of virtual rewards, such as badges. In and of themselves, badges don't mean anything. They have no inherent value. They're just pixels, after all. But if, say, a badge were rewarded to recognize a behavior that was difficult to perform, or to reflect a certain level of effort on the part of the user, your users will find it valuable. The badge represents something to the audience — how hard they worked, or their level of expertise or commitment. It's something that tells the story of their growth.

Of course, not *all* badges require some Herculean effort; some, such as those meant to entice new users to participate, will be easy to earn. But to keep users engaged with your gamification program over the long haul, you'll need to be sure to include more meaningful rewards.

Figure 5-12:
This collection of badges ties in nicely with the main thrust of the site: watching videos.

Image courtesy of Badgeville

Choosing rewards

Chapters 3 and 4 explore some common business objectives and behaviors that help drive those objectives. To refresh your memory, here are some examples of these key behaviors:

- Voting on content
- Asking a question
- Sharing an idea
- Resolving an issue within five business days
- Responding to a lead within 24 hours
- Completing a training course

All these are examples of behaviors — both simple and advanced — that, depending on your business objective, you will want to reward.

Wait until the desired behavior is complete before rewarding it. For example, don't reward a user for clicking a button to start playing video; reward him for watching it to the end.

The question, naturally, is what type of rewards will best suit your gamification program? That, friends, is the $64 million question. O, were that we could provideth you with a simple answer — but unfortunately, we can't. You'll have to do a bit of thinking, considering multiple factors to determine what style of reward will reap the desired benefits. These factors include the following:

- Cost
- The degree of sociability
- Context and value
- Customer relationship management (CRM) life cycle
- Valued versus valuable behaviors

Rewarding behavior is a dynamic process. What you're rewarding today could be different from what you might reward in a month or two.

Addressing cost

Obviously, if your budget is more Mary Lou Retton (small) than Rulon Gardner (large), you'll want to opt for a less-expensive rewards program. That probably means focusing more on recognition and privileges than on monetary rewards.

Even if your budget falls on the Rulon Gardner end of the spectrum, low- cost rewards may still be the way to go. It all depends on what you are trying to achieve with your rewards program.

Indeed, many recognition- and privileges-based rewards are free. Take badges, for example. Yes, you may have to pay someone to come up with a clever name and a catchy design, but after that, they're nothing more than pixels on a screen. Free! Likewise, many privileges — for example, offering your best customers early access to sales or products — involve zero expense. Not so monetary rewards. Whether they're discounts, free shipping, prizes, or redemptions, monetary rewards involve either lost revenue or a cash outlay.

As mentioned, if you do opt to go the monetary rewards route — specifically, offering prizes or redemptions — stick with items you have on hand or in stock, or that broadcast your brand.

Social versus solo

If your site is social in nature — like an online weight loss site or, say, a forum for the foremost authorities on Lionel trains — you'll find that recognition is the best reward. With these types of sites, it's all about status and reputation — badges, levels, and leaderboards. Status and reputation are also key on collaborative sites.

Particularly with social sites, the effects of rewards are amplified because everyone else on the site can be made aware that the reward has been received. This in turn surfaces activity and increases churn in the site's "ecosystem."

It follows, then, that the less social your site is, the less valuable recognition-based rewards will be to your user. In that case, you'll need to rely more on privileges or monetary rewards, as shown in Figure 5-13.

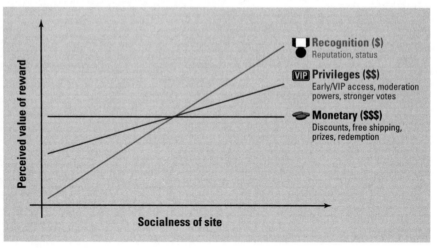

Figure 5-13:
With a highly social experience, you can deliver meaningful, low-cost rewards.

Exploring context and value

As you develop your rewards strategy, your *numero uno* consideration will be the context of your site or business and, by extension, the value it provides to your users or customers. Is it an e-commerce site designed to appeal to value-conscious users? Is it an online community geared toward weight loss? Is it an in-house sales app designed to help your sales team keep track of leads? Is the site social in nature or more of a solo endeavor? Answering these questions will help you determine which type of reward is most appropriate.

Context is also relevant to your products, culture, and services. For example, someone inside a large company might not care about being a "Wiki Contributor" for his or her contributions to the intranet. But they might care deeply about earning "Product Wizard" status for their contributions to the Product wiki specifically.

You should also consider the behavior you're rewarding. How important is it to your organization? How much effort does the behavior require? Behaviors that are particularly important or difficult generally merit a better reward — but what constitutes *better* will again depend on context. For some organizations, a well-designed, clever badge will suffice; others require something tangible.

How users perceive rewards

As you're developing your rewards, one thing to consider is the various ways your rewards might be perceived by your users. Here are a few examples:

✔ **Progress milestone:** Users might see that rewards are a way to measure progress. In this case, each reward should communicate specific information about the goal achieved. That is, there should be a clear story behind the reward — like, "I commented seven times, so I received this reward." Or, "I lost 15 pounds, so I received this reward."

✔ **Discovery temptation:** Sometimes, a reward serves to convey to the user what other rewards can be won — say, by performing additional behaviors or through the discovery of hidden content. This promotes exploration of the site.

✔ **Utility tool:** Rewards such as badges can double as links, acting as a shortcut to a topic of interest. This gives the reward extra utility and provides an extra point of interaction.

✔ **Identity metric:** Rewards can reinforce the user's identity, corroborating who they are — for example, demonstrating how passionate a user is about, say, basketball or basketry. This is especially true with badges, which can be designed and labeled in such a way to speak to a user's personality and interests.

✔ **Social identifier:** Rewards can serve as a means for similar users to find each other — for example, when a badge is displayed to identify a particular interest or area of expertise. For this to work, rewards such as badges should be visible at locations of social contact (comments reviews, leaderboards, and so on).

Considering the CRM life cycle

Depending on where they are in the CRM life cycle, different customers tend to respond to different types of rewards:

✔ **Are you looking to attract new customers or to reengage customers who have lapsed?** If so, you'll probably need to offer monetary rewards to entice them to act. Monetary rewards may also be effective if your aim is to nudge minimally engaged users into becoming moderately engaged users.

✔ **Is your objective to reward your most loyal users?** Odds are, they'd prefer recognition or privileges. After all, they've already demonstrated a willingness to purchase your product or perform good work; plying them with free stuff or giving them a discount probably won't make them *more* willing. Recognition and privileges can also help nudge moderately engaged users into becoming highly engaged users (see Figure 5-14).

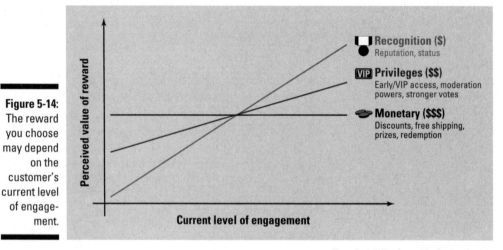

Figure 5-14: The reward you choose may depend on the customer's current level of engagement.

It's all about identifying what motivates users. The users who already see value in your offering want reinforcement that the value they see is meaningful. The users who don't see value need a little enticement to get them in the door; then — they need to be *shown* the value.

Rewarding on the valued/valuable behavior spectrum

In Chapter 4, we talk about valued behaviors versus valuable behaviors. To refresh your memory:

- ✔ **Valued behaviors** are behaviors that your target audience — be they customers or employees — already perform (or would be inclined to perform) because those behaviors have an inherent worth to them.

- ✔ **Valuable behaviors** are behaviors that are important to *you*. They're the ones that drive revenue or growth on your site. They're also the ones that will help you meet the business objectives you've identified for your gamification program.

As we noted, in a perfect world, your target audience's valued behaviors will align perfectly with the behaviors your organization views as valuable.

If they don't align, your goal is to find a way to make it so they do, or at the very least find the middle ground between the two. And that's where rewards come in.

As you build your reward program, you'll want to start by rewarding the behaviors users already perform because they're of some worth to the user. Then, as those rewards gain acceptance, you can layer on rewards for the behaviors you *want* users to perform. If you play your cards right, eventually, those *valuable* behaviors will become *valued* behaviors. That is, they'll become part of the larger, valued experience.

Another approach might be to think of these divergent valued and valuable behaviors as being on a spectrum, with valued behaviors (the ones your users already do) on the right and valuable behaviors (the ones you want to encourage) on the left. The farther to the left you are on that spectrum, the more likely it is you'll need to focus on monetary rewards — something tangible. As you move to the right, however, into behaviors that are valued, or more intrinsic, you can ease into privileges and reputation — more "virtual" (and less costly) rewards (see Figure 5-15). It all depends on how directly you want to pursue those valuable behaviors. If simply increasing overall engagement is enough, stick to the valued behaviors.

Figure 5-15:
As you move toward more valued behaviors, you can ease into more virtual rewards.

Valuable behaviors
Tangible rewards

Valued behaviors
Virtual rewards

Illustration by Wiley, Composition Services Graphics

The more you can get away from rewarding with tangible goods in favor of virtual ones, the better — both from a cost standpoint and from the standpoint of aligning your business objectives with your users' valued behaviors.

If a behavior you encourage is way out of left field, your users probably won't perform — unless your reward is crazy compelling.

Identifying When to Reward

At this point, you've pinpointed your business objectives, determined what behaviors drive those objectives, and what types of rewards you want to give users who engage in those behaviors. This begs the question: When should you give rewards, and how often?

One way to determine when to give rewards is to base it around the natural life cycle of the gamification program. In broad terms, this life cycle consists of the following phases:

- Onboarding
- Mid-game
- Elder-game

Rewarding during the onboarding phase

Not to be confused with the onboarding process undertaken by new hires at an organization (discussed in Chapter 2), the onboarding phase for users of a gamification system is relatively short — maybe one or two sessions. Nevertheless, it is extremely important. After all, this is a new user's intro-duction to your gamification program. During this phase, the user doesn't know anything about the program and has no reason to like it. If anything, the user probably feels a little irritated by the interruption of his or her usual site usage. It's especially crucial, then, to reward users handsomely during this phase.

To catch the user's interest, you need to open with a positive experience. Give the player recognition for a desirable behavior right off the bat — a quick, easy moment of victory. The user's first reward should be easy to obtain — indeed, it should be impossible *not* to obtain it. This accomplishes two things:

- It gets the user off to a positive start.
- It introduces the action-reaction loop.

Use this moment of victory to introduce the system on an up note. Draw attention to the behavior and the reward; connecting the cause and effect is critical. For example, you might display a message such as "Congratulations! By creating an account, you've earned the New Kid badge!" In this way, the user grasps the idea of *if I do this behavior, I get recognition.* The user also sees that this whole feature-tracking business might not be a bad thing.

Once the user understands the connection between behavior and reward, there must be pressure to engage. That is, the user must realize that failing to do so will result in lost progress. An obvious way of conveying this might be through a blatant call to action to preserve the acquired status.

The first award is the most important, but the next few are also critical. They establish scope. Sure, this site tracks visits — but what else does it track? Anything more interesting? Anything more personal?

You should give away at least three rewards per session during this phase.

During this phase, you are essentially selling the user on your system. As you do, the user will naturally be studying how the reward system is integrated into your site. Consciously or not, the user will be wondering:

- ✔ Is my progress surfaced somewhere obvious and accessible?
- ✔ Is my progress/status represented in my social interactions?
- ✔ Does status have benefits?

In case you're unsure, the answers to all these questions should be *yes*. After all, if the site doesn't take the reward system seriously, why should the user?

The user needs to know that a gamification system exists. If the system is hidden — if you're waiting for users to stumble over a first achievement — your program is going to underperform, particularly with new users.

Although you do want to reward users early and often in this phase, you must be careful to avoid diluting the rewards. In other words, don't reward users for every single comment or page view. Eventually, users will view those rewards as being meaningless.

Rewarding during the mid-game phase

Once the user has been convinced and onboarded, the system must continue to delight. That's the objective of the mid-game phase. This phase is all about progress. The user is unlocking achievements and reaching new levels. In other words, experiencing more triumphs.

During this phase, the user must be aware of the path to progress — that is, where to find the next victory. You can build a clear path to progress in three ways:

✔ **Pushing the next step:** Maintain a constant, visible reminder about the next step. After each victory, nudge the user toward what's next (see Figure 5-16). The user should never be allowed to forget that there is a reward still waiting to be to be claimed.

Figure 5-16: Make sure users know what they need to do next to keep winning.

Image courtesy of Badgeville

✔ **Giving users multiple paths toward success.** Providing diverse achievements helps alleviate fatigue and builds more urgency. You want users to think, "I can't leave now — there's still a few things left to do!"

✔ **Incrementing gradually.** Introduce tasks that are gradually more challenging. The previous achievement is a setup for the next achievement. Don't ever allow the user to dismiss the next task as too difficult and don't let too much time pass between victories. At least for the first week or so, your users should be capable of accomplishing at least one achievement every day.

In practical terms, for at least the next ten sessions, the user should feel the taste of victory at least once every session. That doesn't mean that simply logging in drops a reward in the user's lap, but logging in and interacting to a reasonable degree should give the user something — some sense of progress. And all the while, points could be visibly accumulating.

You may want to reward some players for being great community members or loyal fans. In that case, you might opt to manually assign a reward.

Balancing the scale

On the one hand, you want to have rewards to give out for a long time in the future. On the other hand, you want to shower a user in frequent rewards to keep him or her engaged. Unless you have an unlimited quantity of rewards, you're going to have to find a balance.

You'll start out giving away at least three rewards per session, but over time, that will have to change. When it does, users will start to disengage — unless they have made adequate progress or built up enough presence that they feel they'd be throwing something away by leaving.

So how do you know when the user has reached this point where it is safe to ease off on the frequency of rewards? Think about status. Do the stats paint a unique picture? Does the user look different from most everyone else? The answer needs to be yes before you consider slowing down the rewards.

Eventually, the user will need to do more than just reach for the next step on the ladder. They'll need a higher motivation — looking ahead and farther down the line. We call this a *source of aspiration*. You can build a clear source of aspiration in three ways:

- ✔ **Show the full story.** Users need to know where they stand in the community and how far they are from reaching their goals. This might be through interactions with higher-ranking members in the community, a series of leaderboards, or simply revealing the full achievement ladders in a place where everyone can find them. Although the full story shouldn't be central to every interaction on the site, hints of it should be felt throughout the user experience.

- ✔ **Follow through on integration.** Tie benefits to status. Give users real privileges for all their hard work. Reward them with responsibility and deeper forms of interaction. Make them the captains of your site. They've clearly shown their dedication to your site; haven't they earned a little trust?

- ✔ **Keep content first.** In the minds of your users, the reason they're returning to your site is never the rewards; it's their passion for your content. Never make the mistake of placing greater prominence on the rewards than on the content.

The temptation is to design solely for the mid-game phase. Doing so is a mistake, however. You must account for all the phases of the program's life cycle.

Rewarding during the elder-game phase

Eventually, a user gets to the point where he's done everything the site has to offer, many times over. Even though he's built up a large presence, he's still thinking about leaving out of sheer boredom. What to do? Here are three strategies:

✔ **Postpone the inevitable.** Don't let the user finish everything, ever. If you have 10 levels, and it takes four weeks to progress from level 8 to 9, make it take ten weeks to get to level 10. You don't want every collection or progression to be unattainable, but make sure there are a few that basically are.

✔ **Allow new privileges.** In a traditional game, players who beat the game are often rewarded with a new mode. Basically, they get to play the whole game over again with just a few rules changed. While this new version might be harder, the players are often given some new powerful ability. In the same way, you can give your users new privileges — even let them have some control over the site. Let them play the "game" from your side of the table, helping to manage newer players.

✔ **Introduce extensions.** Try introducing new features that are available only to elder users. If no new features are available, consider withholding features from early and mid-game users. At the very least, you should add new achievements with increased requirements that are above and beyond anything you already have.

Throughout the game cycle, rewards must be exciting (read: new), issued frequently, and meaningful to the user. The experience should not be too repetitive; otherwise, users will get bored.

Fixed-rate rewards versus variable ratio reward schemes

Typically, rewards are issued at a fixed rate — i.e., visit ten times, receive a badge. But another approach is to add some randomness to rewards using variable ratio reward schemes. For example, instead of issuing a badge when someone visits 10 times, you could select a range, issuing the badge when someone engages in that behavior somewhere between 8 and 12 times. This randomness could serve to further engage users, who may be pleasantly surprised to receive a reward more quickly than they expected.

That being said, variable ratio rewards schemes are a bit of a Pandora's box. Although they appear simple, these systems are in fact a rather sophisticated game mechanic, requiring a significant amount of balancing. In addition, although they may delight users when rewards are issued on the early side of the range, they could frustrate users when rewards are given late. Perhaps a better approach is to make certain rewards "hidden" — that is, users aren't aware of the reward's existence until they receive it. That way, when a user does receive the reward, she feels unexpected delight. If you've ever seen someone hit the jackpot on a slot machine or watched a child stumble upon a prize during an Easter egg hunt, you've witnessed surprise and unexpected delight in action. Featuring this kind of "serendipitous enjoyment" in your gamification program can go a long way toward fostering engagement. As an added bonus, these hidden rewards drive communication among site members, as in, "Hey! How'd you get that badge?"

Chapter 6

Game On: Understanding Game Mechanics

*G*ame mechanics comprise the components of a game — the tools employed by game designers to generate and reward activity among players. (In the case of a gamification system, "players" refers to customers, employees, or other users.) Game mechanics guide users' behaviors.

It should come as no surprise that world-class companies have begun applying some of the same proven, addictive game mechanics to reward behaviors in non-game environments, both with customers and employees. Indeed, most gamification programs leverage game mechanics in one way or another.

This chapter highlights the key game mechanics you can use in your gamification efforts to incentivize and motivate users to perform valuable behaviors and drive engagement. Although you can certainly use gamification to address big, complex issues, the game mechanics themselves need not be big and complex. So long as it's fun, a simple game system can be incredibly effective — even when addressing massive problems.

Here's the Skinny: A Brief Intro to Game Mechanics

Any good gamification guru will tell you: You're only as good as the tools in your toolbox. When it comes to game mechanics, various tools are available to you — each designed to elicit a specific reaction in players. You can combine these tools in nearly infinite ways to create a broad spectrum of responses and experiences. These tools include the following:

- ✔ Points
- ✔ Leaderboards
- ✔ Levels
- ✔ Missions, challenges, and quests
- ✔ Feedback

You may hear people use the terms *game mechanics* and *game dynamics* interchangeably, but doing so is as wrong as a chocolate-covered cricket. Game mechanics comprise the components of a game. Game dynamics refers to players' interactions with those mechanics.

Get to the Point: Understanding Points

If a tree falls in a forest but no one can hear it, does it make a sound? On a related note, if you successfully perform a task in a game, but you don't receive points for it, did it even happen? The fact is, unless a player receives points during gameplay, he or she may not even be aware that the game is afoot.

Points help users know they're in a gamified environment and that many of the small behaviors they take along the way are being recognized at a system level (see Figure 6-1). Companies running gamification programs use points to spur desired behaviors.

EARN POINTS WITH NEST EGGS Buy Shares with every 100 points you earn.

Become a member		50
Start a profile		20
Post a blog	limit 3 per day	20
Upload a video	limit 3 per day	20
Spin the wheel	limit 3 per day	3
Sign up for WorldShares pledges		10
Sign up for a free eco-conferencing trial (Sponsored by iMeet)		100
Sign up for newsletter		10
Share with Facebook	limit 3 per day	5
Twitter	limit 3 per day	3
Take an RSS feed		3
E-mail a friend	limit 3 per day	10
Make a comment	limit 5 per day	5
Read/rank an article	limit 10 per day	3

Image courtesy of MNN

Figure 6-1:
Points help people understand a game is happening.

In gamification, points are assigned for specific behaviors such as creating an account, signing in, uploading a video, commenting on a thread, mentioning an organization on Facebook or Twitter . . . the list goes on (see Chapter 4 for more). These points can then be compiled into a score.

A word on "fun"

You might think of game mechanics as the stuff in a game that makes the game fun — and a bit addictive. But *why* are games fun? To be honest, the answer to this question is up for debate. Indeed, it's one that game designers just can't agree on. Our view, however, is that games are fun because they offer three things:

✔ **Fantasy:** Imagination, stories, role playing, fiction

✔ **Choice:** Strategy, control, self-expression

✔ **Growth:** Learning, overcoming challenges, making social connections, building a sense of order

Gamification, however, does not address all three of these facets of fun. That is, gamification is not about fantasy. You're not trying to tell users a story. Nor is it about choice, per se. That leaves growth, and that's the key. The game mechanics used in gamification take the growth aspects of games — again, learning, overcoming challenges, making social connections, building order — and put them into your site.

For example, let's say you want to attract more users to your website's forum and increase engagement among existing users. In that case, you might issue points to the following:

✔ Existing users who mention the forum on Twitter

✔ New users who create a user account

✔ Users who log on to the forum

✔ Users who leave a comment

✔ Users who start a thread

Remember from Chapter 4: Ideally, your target audience's *valued* behaviors (the behaviors they perform because they're worthwhile to *them*) should align with the behaviors your organization views as *valuable*. That will result in a seamless experience for the user. As mentioned, if they *don't* align, your goal is to find a way to make them do so.

Weighting points

To really drive desired behaviors, game designers can weight points. *Weighting* points means awarding more points for those behaviors deemed more valuable or that require more effort.

For example, if your business objective is to drive more user-generated content, then it's more important for visitors to create a new blog post rather than simply like an existing one. In that case, you'd weight your point system to favor users who create new blog posts. You might issue 500 points to someone who writes a blog post, but just 50 points to someone who likes an existing post. In this way, you both reward users for performing desired behaviors and indicate to users which behaviors are most valuable to you.

To figure out how to weight points, you first must know your business objective — that is, the specific pain point you want to address. At Samsung, for example, they noticed that although the Web site provided robust user-generated content tools and welcomed millions of users, only a small percentage of those users actually created content or came back on a frequent basis.

To improve retention, Samsung launched an engagement program called Samsung Nation, which focused on rewarding behaviors that required customer time and attention. Samsung opted to reward behaviors based on the behaviors' value to the company and the effort required by the user to complete them:

- ✔ Register Samsung products: 500 points

- ✔ Submit comments and reviews: 300 points

- ✔ Provide answers in Q&A: 300 points

- ✔ Watch videos: 200 points

- ✔ Like on Facebook: 200 points

- ✔ Share on Twitter: 100 points

- ✔ Submit questions in Q&As: 100 points

All this is to say, not all behaviors are created equal. Although posting a question about a product is valuable to Samsung (100 points), it's a lot easier to ask the question than it is to come up with an intelligent answer, which Samsung credits with 300 points.

As you weight points, you may find it useful to be familiar with the Power Law of Participation. As outlined by social media guru Ross Mayfield, the Power Law of Participation deconstructs the idea of participation into more granular behaviors: reading, tagging, commenting, and so forth. Mayfield describes some of these behaviors as *low-threshold* behaviors. They're the ones that are easy to perform and require little in the way of participation. These behaviors might include reading a post, tagging a post, or favoriting a post — all pretty easy. Other behaviors are considered high-threshold. They involve a little more work, like writing, collaborating, or moderating (see Figure 6-2). Assuming they're valuable to your organization, high-threshold behaviors would likely garner higher point values due to the fact that they require more effort to perform.

Figure 6-2:
Ross
Mayfield's
Power Law
of Participa-
tion places
behaviors on
a spectrum.

Image courtesy of Ross Mayfield

When devising your point system, should you go with big numbers or small ones? That is, should users receive 10 points for commenting, or 100? When they upload a video, should they receive 20 points or 200? Often, people prefer big numbers — but before you go that route, make sure your user interface has enough space to support those big-digit numbers.

Keeping context in mind

When it comes to issuing points, companies can also take into account specific content, products, and processes.

For example, rather than just awarding points to someone for commenting anywhere on your site, maybe you just reward them for commenting on a specific item or category. Suppose you really want to drive engagement around a certain topic — say, football. In that case, you might award additional points to users who blog about the next big game. As an added bonus, this would enable you to issue rewards that relate to the topic — for example, a special "Gridiron God" badge.

Identifying point types

Gamification efforts typically employ a few different types of points. These include the following:

> ✔ Experience points
>
> ✔ Redeemable points
>
> ✔ Karma points

You need not limit yourself to one type of points in your gamification efforts. Some designs use multiple types. It all depends on what type of behavior you intend to drive. It also depends on what you want to reward. In some cases, a point unit will contribute to real, extrinsic rewards. In other cases, it'll simply be tied to rank, status, and reputation within a community.

Experience points

Experience points are used in many games to quantify a player's progression through the game. Each time a player performs some type of action in a game system, he or she earns experience points. The more you interact with a game system, the more experience points you earn. Experience points can only go up.

These points typically don't act like currency in the game system — that is, they can't be redeemed for rewards or prizes. Rather, they're the method by which players are ranked within the system. They're also the method by which game designers monitor and guide players. For example, game designers might give players with lots of experience points access to more difficult levels or challenges.

Most gamified systems track experience points — even if players aren't made aware of them. Experience points enable gamemakers to stay abreast of their players and the activities they engage in. This in turn enables those gamemakers to tweak the system for improved outcomes.

A subset of experience points are reputation points — that is, experience points that are awarded only for behaviors in a particular area or subject. In systems that require trust, reputation points are essential; users who score high in reputation points can reasonably be considered trustworthy.

If your system involves reputation points, be on the lookout for players who try to "game" the system and be prepared to implement anti-gaming mechanisms (covered later in this chapter).

Redeemable points

Redeemable points are — wait for it — points that can be redeemed. Maybe players redeem points for a tangible reward, such as a plane ticket. Or maybe they redeem points within the game system itself — for example, to "purchase" a special tool. That's an example of a virtual reward.

Virtual reality: Understanding virtual economies

Redeemable points are at the heart of any virtual economy. A *virtual economy* is a lot like a real economy. Virtual economies involve the use of virtual currency (redeemable points) to purchase virtual goods — say, buying a vowel on your iPhone's Wheel of Fortune app, acquiring Park Place in Monopoly, or buying a bushel of hay in FarmVille.

Although virtual economies tend to pertain more to games than to gamification per se, building a vibrant virtual economy is a great tool if your aim is to incentivize broad behaviors or large communities. As you develop your virtual economy, you'll issue virtual currency to those users who engage in the behaviors you want to encourage, making sure the currency can be used to buy virtual goods that people find appealing.

Tying your efforts to virtual rewards rather than real-world goods lets you reduce marketing and promotion costs by a pretty penny. Think about it: If a user exchanges virtual currency for a real-world good, such as a T-shirt, someone has to purchase that T-shirt and send it to the user. But if the user exchanges virtual currency to buy a virtual item, such as the aforementioned bushel of pixelated hay, all you really give them is some free pixels.

As your virtual economy grows, you can be all Ben Bernanke-like, monitoring and managing the flow of "capital" to match supply with demand. Heads up, though: Virtual economies and the redeemable points that sustain them involve substantial legal and regulatory issues. It might well be a Pandora's box of sorts — one that's just not worth opening.

Unlike experience points, which can only rise, redeemable points can go up or down as users redeem them for rewards. Typically, employing redeemable points will involve integrating the point system with a traditional loyalty program.

Karma points

Some game systems use karma points. For example, suppose you wrote a blog post that another user finds helpful. That other user might give you karma points in the form of a *high five* or a *thumb's up* — whatever unit the site uses. The idea is to promote altruism among users.

A great example of karma points in action can be found on Reddit, a social news Web site where users submit content and other users *upvote* it or *downvote* it. These votes rank the content and ultimately determine the content's position on the site's pages. Content receiving the most upvotes — or karma points — rises to the top, with the top content appearing on the site's home page.

Similar to karma points are gifting mechanisms, which enable users to distribute wee virtual gifts to others on the site — for example, a virtual birthday cake or some digital jewelry.

Exploring multiple point systems

It may be that your system will benefit from the use of a multiple point system. A multiple point system enables you to issue points for behaviors, directing them into different "buckets."

For example, suppose your site awards users 100 points for sharing a review about a product. The site assembles top-scoring users on a leaderboard (discussed in the next section) and enables them to cash in points for, say, free shipping. If you have only one point system, cashing in points means sacrificing the user's rank and status on the leaderboard, which is sure to frustrate those users who enjoy their position at (or near) the top. Having a multiple point system solves this problem. With a multiple point system, you could assign one set of points for redemption and tie another set to the user's lifetime score and reputation.

Follow the Leader: Working with Leaderboards

Winning is great. But you know what's even better? When everyone else knows you won. That's the power of the leaderboard.

The purpose of a leaderboard is to show players where they rank. Those at the top enjoy the notoriety it brings; as for everyone else, the leaderboard shows them where they stand relative to their peers.

Often, the very presence of a leaderboard can elicit the desire to play. The simple goal of rising up the rankings serves as a powerful motivator to continue. People like to keep score. Understanding this and providing easy ways to do it is a great way to foster engagement. For some, the mere sight of their rank on the leaderboard is all the reward they seek.

When it comes to cost-effective gamifying tools, nothing beats a leaderboard.

The trick to leaderboards is designing them in such a way that they encourage players to stay in the game. For example, suppose you have a new user whose current score is 50. She notices on the leaderboard that the top user's score is 1,970,485. She reasonably deduces that if she wants to register the top score, she'll have to neglect her job and family and devote all her waking hours to engaging in the game system. Odds are she will disengage from the system altogether.

Leaderboards should always be encouraging, never discouraging.

One way to head off this scenario is to simply show the player as being smack in the middle of the standings, regardless of where she actually ranks — unless the person actually *is* among the top 10 or 20 players, in which case this should be evident.

Another approach is to *slice* the leaderboard. You can slice leaderboards in several different ways:

- **Locally:** Players see their rank relative to that of others in their geographic area.

- **Socially:** Players see how they stack up against Facebook friends or Twitter followers.

- **By experience level:** Limits the leaderboard such that it displays only those players who have spent a similar amount of time on the site.

- **Contextually:** Sets up the leaderboard to show leaders by category. A content site might display a leaderboard in the business section containing people who contribute in that area, in the fashion section for the top fashionista contributors, and so on.

- **Time:** Sets up the leaderboard to show, for example, weekly or monthly leaders (see Figure 6-3).

Figure 6-3:
You can slice leaderboards to view weekly or monthly leaders.

Leaderboard

★ Weekly   ★ Monthly   ⚑ Overall

Image courtesy of Zurmo

Context can also define the value of a leaderboard. That is, leaderboards with a defined end show who's "winning," whereas leaderboards with no end show "status."

Level Up: Exploring Levels

Anyone who has ever played Donkey Kong or Pac Man (or, for that matter, pretty much any electronic arcade game ever) is familiar with the concept of levels. After you conquered one level, you moved on to the next one. Each level constituted a sub-game of sorts, often with different sorts of obstacles and tools at the player's disposal, and typically becoming more and more difficult.

Levels serve two important roles in gamification systems:

- ✔ **They indicate progress:** Proceeding from one level to the next gives players a sense of satisfaction.

- ✔ **They convey status:** A player who has reached level 42 of your system can reasonably be considered more expert than someone who has failed to advance beyond level 7.

A gamified experience doesn't employ levels in quite the same way as arcade games. If your goal is to gamify a web forum, users won't, for example, suddenly see their whole screen change to offer a new set of challenges the moment they *level up*. Instead, gamified systems more closely mirror roleplaying games such as Dungeons & Dragons, where a level is effectively a rank that corresponds to the player. It's earned through accomplishments and represents additional privileges or abilities.

So if players don't level up by rescuing a princess from a giant gorilla, how *do* they level up in a gamification system? In a gamified system, the change in level occurs when the user reaches a set point threshold, indicated by the reward of a new badge (see Figure 6-4). Or maybe the user gets access to *gated* content (content not available to the poor schlubs on lower levels) or special privileges (first dibs on new products or access to special sales). In this way, users are encouraged to complete tasks and achieve goals.

Figure 6-4:
In gamification, a change in level occurs when the user reaches a point threshold, often resulting in a new badge.

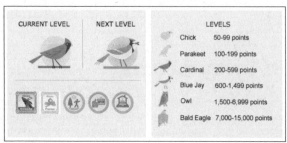

Image courtesy of MNN

Typically, players advance to a new level when they earn a certain number of points. For example, after a player earns his first 100 experience points, he might be bumped up from the first level to the second, and bumped to the third level after crossing the 250-point threshold.

Whatever approach you take, levels should be logical to the player. They should also be extensible. That is, you should design the system such that additional levels can be added over time.

Rather than advance players to the next level in a linear fashion — every 100 points or whatever — opt for a curvilinear approach. That is, start with 100 points, then go to 250, then bump up to 500, and so on. This helps keep players engaged and endows each new level with even more significance.

In gamified systems, naming levels so that they convey the player's status to other users in the system is essential. Each player's level should be displayed, along with her headshot or avatar, throughout the system. If appropriate in your industry, opt for names that are fun — for example, New Kid for new players or Know It All for experienced ones.

Mission Control: Using Missions, Challenges, and Quests

Missions, challenges, and quests are essentially different words for the same thing. They require users to perform a prescribed set of actions, following a guided path of your design. A mission, challenge, or quest might involve a single step (for example, creating an account on your Web site) or several steps — even as many as 20. Often, missions are about discovery or education (see Figure 6-5).

Figure 6-5:
Missions, challenges, and quests guide users down a path to complete a prescribed set of actions.

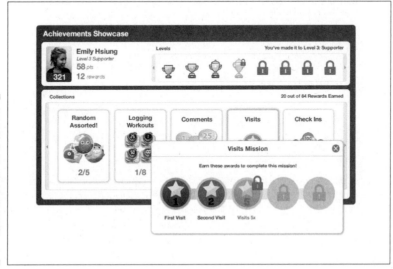

Image courtesy of Badgeville

Mission basics

Sometimes, the actions in a mission must occur in a certain order. These missions are called *progression missions*. Other times, actions can occur in any order. These are called *random missions*. The tasks in a mission might revolve around the same behavior (reading five posts, for example), or could be an around-the-world variety, where different behaviors are performed (for example, reading a post, commenting on a post, and adding your own post).

As each action is completed, users are generally given a reward. The user is also given a reward — usually status-based — when the mission is complete. At the same time, the next mission is unlocked. Successive missions contain harder-to-earn rewards (see Figure 6-6).

Image courtesy of Badgeville

Figure 6-6: As you complete missions, you unlock rewards.

From the player's point of view, completing missions is a lot like leveling up in a particular topic. As players complete each mission, their perceived status will likely increase.

A *track* is a collection of missions. Like missions, tracks can be ordered or unordered, although if the track centers around expertise, then ordered tracks are the way to go. Why? Because the ordered progression of missions represents increasing mastery or advancement in a particular topic or specialization. In other words, the user must complete the first mission before progressing to the second mission, and so on.

Unless your goal is immediate disengagement — which, let's face it, is unlikely — you should not place newbie players into advanced-level missions and tracks. Always develop different challenges for different levels.

You can design missions, challenges, and quests for single players or for cooperative groups. Although the single-player model is easier to design and support, cooperative designs can be more powerful in a social sense. If you have a boatload of active players, consider the cooperative approach. Alternatively, tweak your single-player design to work in a group setting. For example, set it up so that users play alone but their score is combined with others'. For more about team-type missions, see Chapter 10.

You can spice up a mission, challenge, or quest by turning it into a contest where you reward those who finish most quickly or effectively. Typically, contests involve a time frame — in other words, an expiration date. Maybe users need to finish the mission by a certain date. If they do, they win a prize. Or maybe completing the quest in the set time period makes them eligible for entry in a sweepstakes. Contest prizes might include early access to products, discounts, or other privileges. Speaking of prizes, scarcity and exclusivity are often factors when it comes to contests. For example, the prize could be a limited-edition item that's unavailable to others.

Exploring Activity Feeds and Notifications

One way to encourage engagement is to broadcast well-written, helpful, engaging on-screen messaging in the form of real-time notifications within the game system and/or via e-mail when users perform a desired behavior, level up, unlock a reward, or need to complete an additional behavior in order to earn their *next* reward.

Notifications might appear in the user's activity feed or as a small pop-up on the screen (Figure 6-7 shows examples of both) and can become increasingly sophisticated, triggered by any behavior or series of behaviors. Often — especially in game systems that involve daunting goals (for example, on sites devoted to losing weight or mastering a foreign language) — feedback can keep players from feeling paralyzed, as if no progress is being made.

Figure 6-7:
Boost engagement with activity feeds and notifications.

Image courtesy of Badgeville

Specifically, you'll want to provide the following types of feedback:

- ✔ **Behavior hints:** These hints should be short descriptions of what the user needs to do. You don't need to include the result of the action, just the behavior. Examples of behavior hints might be "Visit daily" or "Read articles."

- ✔ **Activity stream text:** This text appears in pop-up notifications known as *croutons*. Examples might include "John read [name of article]" or "Mary commented on [title of video]."

- ✔ **Achievement hints:** Hints for achievements and advanced rewards should provide a short description of what the user needs to do and include how many times the task needs to be done. Some good examples include "Visit 20 times" and "Read 50 articles in the Cars category."

- ✔ **Achievement messages:** What goes in these messages — which should be snappy and engaging — is largely up to you. We recommend something along the lines of "Public Speaker Achievement Unlocked for leaving 20 comments! Has someone been taking classes?"

- ✔ **Level hints:** These hints should tell the user how many points are needed to reach the level. So, "Score 50 points" is a good example.

- ✔ **Level messages:** This should be friendly and engaging text relating to the new level. We recommend reminding the player how many points were scored to reach the level — something like "You scored 500 points and reached the level of 'Authority'!"

- ✔ **Mission hints:** These hints explain what a user should do to complete a mission. Often, this information will already have been conveyed through achievement hints, so you could use these to simply say something fun or encouraging.

- ✔ **Mission messages:** These are congratulatory messages for completing the mission. We suggest the message reference the behavior that was used, but this is optional (see Figure 6-8).

Figure 6-8: Make it clear to users where they are in a mission.

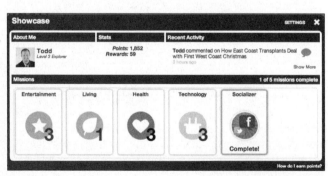

Image courtesy of Badgeville

Don't go crazy on notifications or you'll likely overwhelm your user. For exam-ple, if you run a content site, notifying users when someone comments on or likes a blog post they wrote would be appropriate. Notifying users each time someone *viewed* the post would not be.

Defining the Context

The *context* of a game or gamification system is simply its implied set of rules and values. Although not technically a game mechanic, it does include the dimensions of the game and the reasons for playing. Evidence of this context is in the fact that you might do something in a game you'd never do in real life — like run up and down a grass field for an hour or spontaneously whoop and shout and dance in a circle in front of complete strangers. Sometimes the context is even literally addressed, like when a child playing a game calls time out and tries to temporarily put the game context on hold.

In the case of gamification, a context already exists. Imagine a website. It already has an inherent purpose, a value proposition that draws visitors. This is the site's context, and it exists with or without the addition of gamifi-cation. Proper gamification doesn't strive to bring a new context to the site. It doesn't create a self-contained game on top of or beside the pre-existing site. Rather, it strives to build a game *around* the existing site. The intent should be to enhance the value proposition and deepen the existing context.

 With smart gamification, the primary value of the site doesn't change. Neither do the primary user behaviors or objectives. It's important to recognize that the site's visitors did not come to play a game; they came to interact with the site. Gamification is about using your existing context.

Gamification, when done right, supports and enhances the natural context of the site. It measures valued behaviors. It sets goals. It recognizes accomplish-ments. It opens windows of visibility between like-minded visitors and makes valuable suggestions. For gamification to succeed, the natural values of the site must be a constant consideration during the design process. In other words, the design has to respect the context.

Exploring Anti-Gaming Mechanics

Sadly, people are jerks. (Not you, obviously.) Which is why you can rest assured that at least one bozo out there will try to *game* your system — that is, attempt to cheat or to earn points by exploiting loopholes.

For example, suppose you offer a free T-shirt to all users who earn 10,000 points. Suppose further that users receive 10 points for each page view. Users might attempt to game your system by simply clicking page after page after page. They're not really doing what you want them to do — reading the content, interacting with it — they're just clicking to increase their points.

Fortunately, you can apply various anti-gaming mechanisms to thwart them. Don't worry — unlike with matter and anti-matter (not to mention pasta and antipasti), applying game mechanics alongside anti-gaming mechanics won't cause an explosion. But it will enable you to prevent users from gaming your system.

No matter how smart you are, you won't be able to predict and defend against every type of exploit of your system, especially in the early design stages. Overthinking the issue at the outset will likely result in a pretty boring gamification system. Just be aware of the issue and give yourself room to incorporate anti-gaming mechanics over time.

Following are a few anti-gaming mechanics to consider:

- Cool downs
- Rate limiting
- Count limiting

In addition to these approaches, you can also manually remove points from problem players' totals and remove problem players from your leaderboards. (That'll learn 'em!) You can also set up your system to measure behaviors that are harder to fake — for example, receiving votes from other users.

Implementing cool downs

If you follow IndyCar racing, you may be familiar with the *push to pass* feature. When a driver presses the push-to-pass button on his steering wheel, the car receives extra horsepower for a few seconds, enabling the driver to pass the car ahead (or defend against one creeping up from behind). So, what's stopping the driver from pressing that button all the time? Simple. IndyCar officials implemented a cool-down mechanism. After the button has been pressed, drivers must wait a certain period of time before pressing it again.

A similar approach is used as an anti-gaming measure. With cooldowns, you wait a certain period of time before rewarding a behavior. For example, if you reward users for visiting a page, you might require a 30-second gap between each page view. This increases the likelihood that users are actually doing what you want them to do — in this case, reading the content on the page.

Rate-limiting players

Using that same push-to-pass example, IndyCar officials took further steps to ensure that drivers didn't spend all their time with their fingers on the push-to-pass button by limiting the number of times they could press it per race (or in some cases limiting the total amount of time per race the button could be depressed).

Similarly, to prevent users from gaming your system, you might limit the number of times you reward a behavior over a certain period of time. For example, you might decide to reward players 10 points for each view — but you might limit the number of points rewarding that behavior to 50 per day, 20 per hour, 10 per minute, or what have you. Of course, this approach does have a negative aspect, in that it could discourage users for accessing additional content; you'll have to strike a balance.

 To encourage users to access different areas of content on your site, you could set things up such that the count limit is specific to a particular area of the site. That is, he could receive as many as 50 points for reading articles about business, as many as 50 additional points for reading articles about the arts, and so on.

Count-limiting players

Another option is to limit the total number of times a user is rewarded for performing a certain behavior, ever. For example, you could set things up such that users receive a reward for visiting a particular page just once.

 Suppose your site has a gajillion users who perform a decagajillion behaviors per day. Even if your system is automated to flag bad behavior, one measly admin won't be able to police every little exchange. In that case, you can rely on your community to flag this type of nonsense for you. In fact, you might even make the attainment of Community Sheriff status a reward of sorts. Although this isn't an anti-gaming mechanism per se, it is a tactic you can use to combat hooliganism on your site.

The leaky bucket algorithm

Some gamification programs use a "leaky bucket" algorithm to control the allocation of rewards for behaviors performed. This algorithm features two key parameters: bucket max capacity and bucket drain rate. The *bucket max capacity* is the maximum behaviors credited per hour. Each behavior adds 1 point to the bucket. When the bucket is full, the user is no longer credited for performing behaviors until the bucket begins to drain. The *bucket drain rate*, then, is the number of points that are drained from the bucket over the course of an hour. This draining happens evenly throughout the hour.

By finding the right combination of bucket max capacity and bucket drain rate, you can prevent normal users from running into rate limitations but block users who are trying to game the system. For example, suppose your bucket max capacity is 10 activities per hour, and your bucket drain rate is 5 activities per hour (or once every 12 minutes). When users first visit the site, they can be credited for performing 10 behaviors as quickly as they want. But once the bucket is full (after 10 behaviors), they will only be able to commit an activity once every 12 minutes.

Part II

Decisions, Decisions: Choosing a Gamification Framework

The 5th Wave   By Rich Tennant

Sam Confuses A Gamification Framework With A Gaming Platform

"I really don't know what this is doing to help improve our business, but it's the best project I've ever worked on."

In this part . . .

Maybe you want to use gamification to increase customer engagement. Or perhaps your goal in gamifying your business is to encourage collaboration among employees. Either way, your next step is to determine just *how* to implement gamification. To aid in this, we've identified six gamification frameworks — holistic programs designed to achieve specific business objectives. In this part, you'll get the lowdown on each one, with case studies to boot.

Chapter 7

Freeze Frame: Understanding Gamification Frameworks

● ●

In This Chapter

▶ Identifying the six gamification frameworks

▶ Grasping the basics of each gamification framework

▶ Determining which gamification framework is right for your business

● ●

*A*fter much thought, you've decided you want to gamify some aspect of your business to achieve a specific result. Maybe you want to use gamification to increase customer engagement. Or perhaps your goal in gamifying your business is to encourage collaboration among employees.

Your next step is to determine just how to implement gamification. To aid in this, we've identified various gamification frameworks. These frameworks provide a path for getting up and running with a gamification program and help accelerate the aim of the program targeted to achieve a specific goal.

Each of these frameworks responds to a specific business objective, using specific mechanics to help drive the behaviors that pertain to that objective.

Think of frameworks as being like blueprints for building a house. You could try to build a house out of a pile of lumber and supplies, but a blueprint makes the job much easier. The advantage of the blueprint is that it is written by an expert — someone who has built many houses. It guides you through the overwhelming task of building.

A *gamification framework* is a holistic program designed to achieve a specific business objective. The framework you use depends on the outcome you want to achieve.

You can mix frameworks.

Introducing the Six Gamification Frameworks

As you might expect, you have many options in terms of gamification frameworks.

We've identified six broad approaches. As mentioned, each framework is designed to address a specific business need. Some of these frameworks are designed to address an internal (employee-facing) need, whereas others are designed for external (customer-facing) use. Some frameworks work best in solo environments (for an individual); others are ideal for collaborative settings (for a community); and still others speak to competitive arenas (say, a gaming site).

The six gamification frameworks are as follows (also see Figure 7-1):

- **Social loyalty:** This framework is for customer-facing experiences that occur in nonsocial environments, such as a traditional e-commerce experience. This framework focuses on rewards.

- **Community expert:** This framework is for customer-facing experiences that rely on quality user-generated content and contributions. This framework focuses on reputation.

- **Competitive pyramid:** This framework is for customer-facing communities that seek to motivate competitive behavior. This framework focuses on status and score.

- **Gentle guide:** This framework guides employees through a process. This framework focuses on ensuring completion and compliance.

- **Company collaborator:** This framework is designed to increase contributions by employees, developers, and partners in internal communities.

- **Company challenge:** This framework is designed to challenge your staff to compete on teams to encourage high-value behaviors.

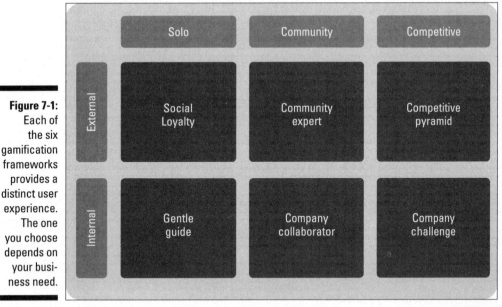

Figure 7-1:
Each of the six gamification frameworks provides a distinct user experience. The one you choose depends on your business need.

Matching a Framework to Your Business Objective

The six basic frameworks cover the six basic goals — three for customer-facing applications and three for employee-facing ones — that most companies are aiming to achieve.

The three most popular goals for customer-facing sites are as follows:

- ✔ Increased adoption
- ✔ Increased community involvement
- ✔ Increased competition

And here are the three most popular goals for employee-facing sites:

- ✔ Increased low-level employee engagement (task management)
- ✔ Increased high-level employee engagement (creative cooperation)
- ✔ Increased company-wide goal-setting

Now align those goals with the appropriate framework:

- **Social loyalty:** Increased adoption
- **Community expert:** Increased community involvement
- **Competitive pyramid:** Increased competition
- **Gentle guide:** Increased low-level employee engagement (task management)
- **Company collaborator:** Increased high-level employee engagement (creative cooperation)
- **Company challenge:** Increased company-wide goal-setting

The frameworks are just a starting point. From each of these basic approaches, additional details are added to target more specific goals, such as onboarding, currencies, social mechanics, and so on.

Comprehending the Social Loyalty Framework

The social loyalty framework is classic gamification. It's all about increased adoption. If you find yourself trying to engage the masses who are "just passing through" or you would like to convert a one-time customer into a returning one, then the social loyalty framework is for you.

This framework takes what your site's users already do — their *valued behaviors* (think visiting, browsing, sharing, purchasing, and so on) — and uses gamification to increase engagement and activity (see Figure 7-2). This framework is highly flexible and can be implemented in many ways.

Figure 7-2:
Rewards, such as badges, are one tool leveraged by the social loyalty framework to engage users.

Image courtesy of Badgeville

Examples of types of businesses that might benefit from the social loyalty framework include the following:

- **Retail and e-commerce:** Retail marketers want increasing conversions and retention. The social loyalty framework helps increase the behaviors users engage in on your site. It lets you guide shoppers to content and increase retention and conversions.

- **Entertainment:** You can use this framework to boost fan advocacy and loyalty for entertainment brands. It lets you measure and reward loyalty and encourages viral advocacy.

- **Conferences, events, live experiences:** This framework is ideal for live events and experiences, such as conferences, with activities managers want attendees to perform. It can motivate conference attendees to check-in to sessions and visit booths on a trade show floor, for example, to complete a mission and receive a reward.

Why does the social loyalty framework work? Here are a few reasons:

- **Recognition:** A major reason it's effective in many communities is the essential human desire for acknowledgement. Recognition for achieving a task or accomplishing a goal not only feeds this human need but encourages engagement and increases repetition of valued (and valuable) behaviors.

- **Visualization of progress:** Through simple feedback (points, leaderboards, levels, achievements, badges, and so on), users receive clear guidance as to what they've achieved and what else they need to do to move forward. This visualization of where they've been and where they're going is instrumental.

- **Rewards:** Rewards are valuable to all users, whether they're driven by monetary incentives, privileges, or recognition. Using this framework, all types of rewards can be easily leveraged.

You'll learn more about the social loyalty framework in Chapter 8.

Experts Only: Exploring the Community Expert Framework

The community expert framework is for online communities that want to establish user reputation hierarchies. These hierarchies serve to stroke the egos of active users and to connect users who need help with those who can provide it.

This framework rewards your site's users for what they already do (their valued behaviors) and lets them complete missions and level-up in relevant categories of expertise. The result? Quality contributions and identifiable experts.

By highlighting reputable contributors, the community expert framework improves the quality of content filtering and facilitates user-to-user connections. When your active community members and top content creators are rewarded with status, their output increases, improving the overall quality of your site experience (see Figure 7-3).

Figure 7-3:
Rewarding active community members and top content creators with status improves the overall quality of your site experience.

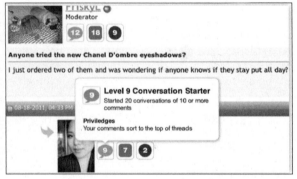

Image courtesy of Badgeville

Examples of types of businesses that might benefit from the community expert framework include the following:

- **Publishing media (blogs, newspapers, magazines):** Users leave more quality comments when they receive community status for these valuable contributions.

- **Crowdsourcing (Q&A, creative, reviews):** Traditionally performed by specific individuals to a group of people or community, crowdsourcing works well with the community expert framework because users are quickly identified for their expertise and social standing.

✔ **Discussion communities and forums:** This framework provides a meaningful way for users to improve their status and reputations for participating with quality contributions, improving content and increasing user interconnectivity.

Why does the community expert framework work? Here are a few reasons:

✔ **Identity:** Recognition of who the user is, what expertise the user carries, and what social standing the user has is important to creating a natural hierarchy within the community. The distinguishing character or personality of an individual is showcased, leading to desirable engagement and increased community participation.

✔ **Relevance:** Instead of users sifting through pages of content to find stuff, the community expert framework showcases the expertise of all players, related to all topics, so the material a user needs is more immediately discoverable.

✔ **Status:** Within a social environment, the relative position of an individual compared to others is important. Status — and the rewards or privileges that come with it — are valuable to the user because of the sense of worth and pride that comes with an increased standing in a community of their peers.

You'll learn more about the community expert framework in Chapter 8.

Pyramid Power: Pondering the Competitive Pyramid Framework

The competitive pyramid framework supercharges an existing competitive experience by extending the thrill of competition to all aspects of interaction and offering more ways for your users to win.

This framework, similar to Xbox Live's popular achievement model, expands the competitiveness of an activity by creating a pyramid of challenges (see Figure 7-4).

Figure 7-4:
The com-
petitive
pyramid
framework
expands the
competitive-
ness of an
activity by
creating a
pyramid of
challenges.

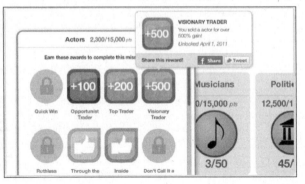

Image courtesy of Badgeville

At the lowest level are dozens of new mini challenges that test a wide variety of skills. The next level up features categorical scores that compare players' skills in particular specializations. At the top level is a site-wide competition that compares players' point totals across all categories.

The competitive pyramid framework is designed for existing game-like experiences, such as traditional online/social games and prediction communities.

Examples of types of sites that might benefit from the pyramid challenge framework include the following:

✔ **Test and quiz sites:** Great for communities that offer tests and quizzes in a competitive environment, it supports a bigger game connecting smaller performance wins.

✔ **Prediction communities:** The competitive pyramid framework is a powerful way to boost user contributions. It lets users compare points across categories and celebrate the best contributors.

✔ **Games and social gaming:** This framework offers an Xbox Live kind of achievement, adding challenges throughout the community to guide engagement and ongoing participation.

Why does the competitive pyramid framework work? Here are a few reasons:

✔ **Competition:** A contest for a prize, badge, or honor, is one of the oldest forms of recreation. Users already in a game environment have proven that they like to win. With even more opportunities to compete and win, players are more deeply engaged and challenged by the variety of competitions.

✔ **Specialization:** By pursuing a particular skill or expertise, a user is able to focus her efforts and increase the chances of victory against a broad competitive base. Victory feeds ambition for further victory and encourages players to expand into further specializations, creating a continuous cycle of victory and engagement.

✔ **Challenges:** Users are kept stimulated when new objectives arise. When there are multiple game layers to an experience, with multiple areas to level-up and win, players are motivated to stay engaged. With multiple game layers to a site, users maintain higher levels of interest and involvement.

You'll learn more about the competitive pyramid framework in Chapter 8.

Break It to Me Gently: Identifying the Gentle Guide Framework

The gentle guide framework is designed to help employees complete a process of steps, such as the everyday tasks of their jobs or a specific, process-oriented training program for required certifications.

With the gentle guide framework, you keep employees task oriented by assigning them a daily mission of objectives. Even the most repetitive or complex jobs are simplified and made manageable with focused, step-by-step rewards (see Figure 7-5).

Figure 7-5: With the gentle guide framework, rewards make even the most repetitive or complex jobs manageable.

Image courtesy of Badgeville

This hand-holding type of framework, used to motivate and incentivize users, is a well-conditioned, successful gamification framework custom-made to reduce the overhead of managing employees in large corporations, as well as reward employees for completing required activities and processes on time.

Examples of types of business areas that might benefit from the gentle guide framework include the following:

- ✔ **Performance management:** The gentle guide lets you measure and reward job performance by tracking behaviors. That makes it a good fit for keeping track of long-term progress and awarding bonuses. It's also good for employees who need motivation or reminders. It can help with timely completion of required employee activities.

- ✔ **Health and wellness:** This framework is often a good choice for sites and apps that focus on users staying on track with a health or wellness program.

Why does the gentle guide framework work? Here are a few reasons:

- ✔ **Baby steps:** Larger, overwhelming tasks are broken down into smaller, easily accomplished micro-tasks. Each micro-task then becomes a little victory and the larger task is no longer overwhelming.

- ✔ **Visualization of progress:** By providing visual measures of progress (via points, checklists, and badges), users receive clear feedback when they perform a desirable behavior. This visualization of where they've been and where they're going is instrumental in keeping your users engaged and performing.

- ✔ **Positive reinforcement:** Instead of punishment or reprimand, positive reinforcement has been proven to result in lasting behavioral modification. Thus, when continuing to successfully accomplish a task and receive recognition, users are further motivated to continue and keep performing towards their short-term and long-term goals.

You'll learn more about the gentle guide framework in Chapter 9.

In Good Company: Understanding the Company Collaborator Framework

The company collaborator framework is used internally to help connect problems with solutions. This framework benefits any company that is large enough that the specific skills of each coworker might not be known corporate-wide.

Employees in need are directed to experts in the problem they're experiencing, while employees, developers, and partners who show proficiency in particular areas level-up in those categories of expertise. They are awarded badges that signify expertise to others and that show up in comment threads or anywhere else employees interact, becoming an integral piece of an employee's identity (see Figure 7-6).

Experts can be sorted and browsed by category to facilitate finding the right person to answer a particular question.

Figure 7-6: In the company collaborator framework, employees are awarded badges that signify their expertise.

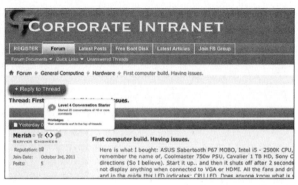

Image courtesy of Badgeville

Examples of types of environments that might benefit from the company collaborator framework include the following:

- ✔ **Internal corporate communities:** The company collaborator framework is good for larger companies with community forums. It can help make better connections between employees.

- ✔ **Developer and partner communities:** This framework can also work with external communities, such as developers and partners. It's aimed at helping users help each other.

- ✔ **Internal wikis:** It's good for giving reputation and rewards to employees who provide content for and share internal wikis. The framework can highlight the most helpful employees among their teams and departments in larger corporations.

Why does the company collaborator framework work? Here are a few reasons:

- ✔ **Identity:** Recognition of who the user is, what expertise the user carries, and what social standing the user has is important to creating a natural role for everyone within the community. Showcasing individual values leads to increased community participation within the workplace.

- ✔ **Relevance:** Instead of users having to shift through pages of content or asking employees from cube to cube, the company collaborator framework organizes the expertise of all employees in the company, making searches quick and relevant. Quickly connecting problems with the appropriate solutions increases productivity and reduces frustration and incorrect information.

- ✔ **Status:** Within a working environment, recognition of an individual's value is important. Status and the rewards or privileges that come with it provide a sense of worth, pride, and job satisfaction.

You'll learn more about the company collaborator framework in Chapter 9.

1 Challenge Thee: Exploring the Company Challenge Framework

The company challenge framework adds a layer of competition to redundant or prescriptive tasks, ranking individual employees or teams of employees according to performance. This friendly layer of competition allows different groups within the company to compete against each other, not only motivating employees and increasing productivity, but also making work more fun.

The company challenge framework is great for building company motivation. Ideal for companies that already have defined teams, this framework has the ability to not only track job performance of each employee, but also to track the performance of an entire team.

Leaderboards compare individual and team performance, awards represent successful task completion, and missions act as daily checklists to complete for rewards and status (see Figure 7-7).

Figure 7-7:
Leader-
boards
compare
individual
and team
performance,
awards
represent
successful
task comple-
tion, and
missions
act as daily
checklists.

Image courtesy of Badgeville

Examples of areas that might benefit from the company challenge framework include the following:

✓ **Sales productivity:** Increase it by adding the company challenge framework to CRM systems. This framework lets you create competition for sales and marketing team members, increasing sales efficiency and revenues.

✓ **Support/call center operations:** This framework is good for support and help-desk systems. With competition for support ticketing systems, employees get a fun, game-like experience for closing more tickets.

✓ **Team performance management:** This framework is perfect for teams at large corporations that have specific metrics for success. The framework increases productivity and encourages teamwork with friendly competition.

Why does the company challenge framework work? Here are a few reasons:

✓ **Visualization of progress:** Clearly measured metrics provide actionable feedback. By providing points, leaderboards, levels, achievements, and badges to reward employee tasks, users receive clear feedback about what they've achieved and what they need to do to level-up. This visualization of performance status is instrumental in keeping employees engaged and performing.

✓ **Rewards:** Rewards are valuable to all users, whether they're driven by monetary incentives, privileges, or recognition. Using the company challenge framework, employee behaviors can be set by team and individual rewards.

You'll learn more about the company challenge framework in Chapter 9.

Take Your Pick: Pinpointing Which Framework Meets Your Needs

So which gamification framework is right for you? That depends entirely on what your needs are.

If, for example, your goal is to increase customer loyalty for your retail or e-commerce site, then the social loyalty framework is best. If, on the other hand, you seek to increase sales performance and productivity, then the company challenge framework is a better fit.

Table 7-1 shows a breakdown of gamification frameworks by industry and goal to help you determine which framework is right for you.

Table 7-1   Gamification Frameworks by Industry

Sample Industry	Sample Goal	Social Loyalty	Gentle Guide	Community Expert	Company Collaborator	Competitive Pyramid	Company Challenge
Retail and e-commerce	Customer loyalty, conversions	X					
Employee training and certification	Education, onboarding		X				
Crowdsourcing, Q&A communities	Quality contributions, community votes			X			
Health and wellness	Health challenges, workouts logged		X				
Employee and developer forums	Increase employee contributions				X		
Entertainment	Fan advocacy	X					
Conferences, events, tourism	Educating users about a schedule or things to do	X					
Sales productivity and team performance management	Sales productivity and performance across a team						X
Games and social gaming	Communities across game experiences					X	
Media, blogs, newspapers	Increase comments and pages read			X			
Internal wiki	Recognize top contributors of company content				X		
Support/help desk	Close tickets more efficiently						X
Individual performance management	Improve employee performance		X				

Chapter 8

Customer-Facing Frameworks

Chapter 7 explains that three of the six gamification frameworks are *external*, or geared toward customer-facing experiences.

This chapter explores these three external gamification frameworks in greater detail:

- ✔ The social loyalty framework
- ✔ The community expert framework
- ✔ The competitive pyramid framework

Exploring the Social Loyalty Framework

Customer-facing and solo in nature (see Figure 8-1), the social loyalty framework is ideal for engaging the masses or converting one-time customers into returning ones. The social loyalty framework rewards your site's or app's users for what they already do: their valued behaviors, such as visiting, browsing, sharing, purchasing, and the like.

Figure 8-1:
The social
loyalty
framework
is customer-
facing and
solo in
nature.

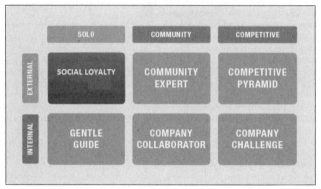

Image courtesy of Badgeville

The social loyalty framework is for specific tasks — from training, certifications, and special promotions to loyalty economies, gamified events, and tradeshows. This framework is all about tracking a variety of goals in parallel. Tasks have a beginning, a middle, and an end, and users are encouraged along the way, making progress, completing sets, and collecting accomplishments.

Let's review the mechanisms by which the social loyalty framework works:

- **Recognition:** Humans have a basic need to be recognized for achievement. Recognition not only feeds this need but encourages engagement and ups the repeating of your customers' behaviors.

- **Visualization of progress:** Users see what they've already achieved and what needs to happen to move forward. This ability to visualize where they've already been and where they're going is important in keeping them engaged, retaining them, and encouraging them to return again and again.

- **Rewards:** Everyone values rewards — money, privileges, and recognition. The social loyalty framework works great with all types of rewards.

Understanding the social loyalty framework's mechanics

With the social loyalty framework, you can apply any number of mechanics. Actually, you can apply pretty much *any* game mechanic with this framework. To review, here are the various mechanics available to you:

- **Points:** Points allow users to compare disparate activities and reveal the relative value of activities. These points can then be compiled into a score, which acts as a measure of progress, success, and the like.

  Setting limits on points is a good idea if the behavior those points reward is exploitable. For example, you might limit the number of times a person can earn points for a given behavior on a daily or weekly basis to prevent users from gaming your site.

- **Leaderboards:** A leaderboard both shows users where they rank and boosts the desire to "play" in order to rise up through the ranks. Those at the top enjoy the notoriety such accomplishment brings; as for everyone else, the leaderboard shows them where they stand relative to their peers. The bottom line? People like to keep score — and a leaderboard enables them to do that.

- **Levels:** Levels indicate progress and convey status. That is, a player who has reached level 21 can reasonably be considered of a higher status than someone who has failed to advance beyond level 4. Typically, users advance to a new level in a gamified system when they earn a certain number of points.

- **Missions:** A mission requires users to perform a prescribed set of actions, following a guided path of your design. Sometimes, the actions in a mission must occur in a certain order. Other times, they can occur in any order.

- **Feedback:** Feedback refers to the broadcast of real-time notifications when users perform a desired behavior, level-up, unlock a reward, and so on. Another type of feedback is an activity feed, which enables users to see what others on the site or app are doing at the site (see Figure 8-2). This feedback keeps players from feeling paralyzed, as if they're making no progress.

- **Achievements and rewards:** These provide positive reinforcement for high-value behaviors. As we say in Chapter 5, rewards can be divided into three categories: recognition, privileges, and monetary rewards. In the social loyalty framework, you can easily leverage all types of rewards.

In the social loyalty framework, rewards can be either hierarchical or standalone. If they're hierarchical, value and difficulty should increase along the hierarchy. If they're standalone, you should take care to award points according to difficulty.

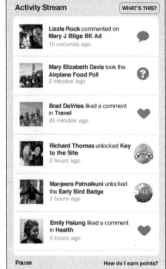

Image courtesy of Badgeville

For more information about each of these mechanics, see Chapter 6.

Identifying popular use cases

As mentioned in Chapter 7, the social loyalty framework is especially useful in certain industries. To review, these include the following:

✔ **Retail and e-commerce:** If you're in this sector, you know a key objective is to increase conversions and retention. Using the social loyalty framework, you can use mechanics such as missions and rewards to guide shoppers to relevant content, increase engagement, improve retention, and increase conversions.

✔ **Entertainment:** The social loyalty framework is excellent for increasing fan affinity and loyalty for all kinds of entertainment brands. Using this framework, you can measure and reward loyalty as well as encourage viral advocacy throughout your community of fans.

✔ **Conferences, events, and live experiences:** This framework is ideal for live events and experiences, such as conferences, where there is a set number of activities that managers would like attendees to perform. For example, suppose your company is organizing a conference, and you want to foster engagement among conference participants. To do so, you could implement social loyalty mechanics — points, leaderboards, missions, rewards, and so on — to spur real-world behaviors, such as checking in at certain booths, trying out demos, attending specific lectures, and so on. The result? Increased engagement during the event itself, a greater likelihood that attendees will come to *next* year's event, and of course, the benefit of any data you manage to gather in the process.

All these use cases employ the basic mechanics of the social loyalty framework — butyou can certainly tune these programs to match up with your own objectives, behaviors, and rewards. In other words, you can adjust these rules to connect best with your specific audience.

Even if your use case doesn't slot in nicely with those listed above, the social loyalty framework may still be appropriate for you. For example, the social loyalty is often the framework of choice, regardless of use case, for the first phase of a gamification program. That is, even if a program will eventually evolve to use a more complex framework, the social loyalty framework is often the best bet at the beginning — especially if you need a simple program and want to be up and running quickly. You can always add the more complex pieces later.

Social loyalty is also best, regardless of use case, if your site or application is customer-facing and nonsocial in nature. That's not to say social loyalty might not work on a social site — just that if your site is *not* inherently social, then social loyalty is probably the way to go.

Finally, you also need to consider whether your site is prescriptive or non-prescriptive in nature. That is, is the site similar to a course curriculum, telling users everything they need to do (prescriptive)? Or can users just run around and pick the things they want to do (non-prescriptive)? If you have a solo, non-prescriptive site, chances are the social loyalty framework is best. Prescriptive sites require a different framework — for example, the gentle guide framework.

Social loyalty framework case studies

This section includes various case studies that demonstrate the effectiveness of the social loyalty framework.

Bell Media

Canadian company Bell Media has significant assets in television, radio, and digital. These include MuchMusic.com (`www.muchmusic.com`), a favorite online destination for youth —sort of like a Canadian MTV.

MuchMusic delivers music videos, user-generated content, and more. Although MuchMusic.com receives millions of visitors a year — and offers plenty of user-generated content tools to engage them — the site needed better ways to reward those users for their participation and to foster more repeat visits.

To improve customer loyalty, the company wanted to tie into a larger marketing campaign of bringing fans "Much Closer" to their favorite artists and celebrities.

MuchMusic.com identified key behaviors across the site that it wanted to influence and eventually reward. These behaviors included the following:

- Signing up
- Leaving a comment
- Uploading content
- Voting on polls
- Liking Much on Facebook
- Tweeting about Much
- Reading an article or blog post on Much
- Visiting the site
- Watching a video
- Sharing a link

For each behavior users performed, Much assigned an appropriate point value. For example, simply visiting a page or reading a blog post was worth 10 points, whereas liking content on Facebook was worth 20 points.

As users accrued points by performing these specific behaviors, they earned different achievements and were rewarded with special privileges and tangible goods in the MuchMusic community, such as an exclusive online chat with cast members from well-known Canadian shows, early access to new content, concert tickets, and more.

MuchMusic.com also used missions — another key game mechanic — to generate engagement with specific shows and campaigns.

Early indications show excellent results:

- 21 percent increase in registered users
- 33 percent of users returning on a daily basis
- 325,000 behaviors performed by users in the first month

Mother Nature Network

Mother Nature Network (www.mnn.com) is an online media site that delivers breaking environmental news from around the Web. Launched in early 2009, the Atlanta-based MNN.com has attracted sponsorship from industry leaders such as GE, AT&T, Coca-Cola, and Mercedes-Benz. It has also partnered with major content distributors including Yahoo!, CNN, and Headline News to promote its online presence.

MNN had a few key challenges it hoped to address for its users:

- ✔ **Social experience:** Although MNN features plenty of rich content and received strong traffic, it faced a common challenge for a site of its kind: It wanted to know more about *who* was visiting and wanted its users to know more about each other, too. This included having them socialize together and interact with site content.

- ✔ **Retention and repeat users:** Because a majority of MNN's visitors were from referrals, many users viewed only one or two articles before leaving. MNN wanted to change these anonymous readers into active, registered members who came back more frequently.

- ✔ **Rewards:** MNN wanted to further engage its current users by rewarding them for exploring and participating on the site.

- ✔ **Sponsorships:** MNN's advertisers create excellent sustainability content for the site, and MNN needed a way to drive more users to those URLs.

To meet these business objectives, MNN sought to drive the following behaviors:

- ✔ Registering for the site
- ✔ Uploading videos
- ✔ Participating in the community
- ✔ Making personal pledges
- ✔ Writing green blog posts
- ✔ Reading articles
- ✔ Signing up for newsletters

To achieve this, MNN embedded game mechanics and social mechanics, including a real-time activity stream, on MNN.com. MNN also launched The Nest, a social loyalty program that enables members to convert their achievements into real donations to participating nonprofits of their choice (see Figure 8-3).

Figure 8-3:
MNN's The Nest lets members convert achievements into donations to nonprofits.

By providing an engaging social experience on top of its rich content, MNN has experienced more engaged users, who return more often. In addition, seeing other users get rewarded for their behaviors has prompted more users to login or signup to get the same rewards, rank, and recognition.

By showcasing an active and growing user base, MNN has attracted more sponsorships of achievements, enabling MNN to both reward customers and increase revenue from advertisers.

sneakpeeq

sneakpeeq, a new kind of e-commerce site, sought to redefine the way people shop and discover emerging brands and products. The San Francisco-based social shopping site makes it easy and fun for customers to connect with millions of up-and-coming style, home, and living brands. It delivers these products on elegantly designed pages for each retailer, where users can interact with beautiful imagery that showcases each item.

While sneakpeeq's ultimate goal was to generate revenue from the sale of high-quality products, the site also wanted to make sure they attracted long-term customers that were highly engaged throughout their lifetimes. Traditional daily-deal and e-commerce sites often failed at this because they had fleeting, one-time buyers who found a particular product once through a search but were never motivated to return. To harness loyal customers, sneakpeeq wanted to reward them for engaging with different elements of the website that improved their overall experience — and drive behaviors they knew would eventually lead to transactions. sneakpeeq also wanted to integrate its social-loyalty program tightly with its Facebook presence, where customers would follow updates about relevant products and new deals on sneakpeeq.

sneakpeeq borrowed proven design and behavioral psychology principles inherent in today's social games to drive desired user behavior and engagement across the site. sneakpeeq identified three critical behaviors that users can perform to show their affinity for different products as they visit different stores on sneakpeeq. These behaviors were:

- ✔ **Share:** Users could share sneakpeeq items on Facebook or Twitter.
- ✔ **Peeq:** When a user visits a product page, she can "peeq" to see a special price.
- ✔ **Love:** A love enables sneakpeeq users to curate their favorite products and display them on their user profiles.

sneakpeeq identified, configured, and assigned point values to these key behaviors and others, including shop clicks, registering, and inviting other users to join. As users share, peeq, and love, they earn points that appear on leaderboards. At the end of every shopping day, top users are rewarded with site credit that can be redeemed at any sneakpeeq store. "The more peeqs and loves customers do throughout the day, the more engaged they are on new products," said Neil Gandhi, sneakpeeq's senior software engineer. "With that level of engagement, we've found they have a much higher likelihood not only to buy, but to frequently return and engage with other sneakpeeq stores."

sneakpeeq gives users discounts for performing specific behaviors on the site. These rewards and achievements are rendered as badges on sneakpeeq user profiles. For example, sneakpeeq created the Monarch badge, which is awarded to people who share their favorite products on sneakpeeq. With each reward, sneakpeeq can assign a specific hint for what users must do to unlock it, and a congratulatory message for when they do.

sneakpeeq has configured hundreds of rewards that users can unlock. With robust rules configuration, sneakpeeq can tie rewards to specific products, content, and stores. For example, instead of merely providing a 20 percent discount for all products across the entire site, sneakpeeq can reward 20 percent for a specific pair of earrings from the newest jeweler, or 30 percent for a pair of shoes at another.

While sneakpeeq focused on engaging customers by driving and rewarding behaviors on the site, it also wanted to pull in more traffic and engagement from users on Facebook. To that end, sneakpeeq began sending key behaviors such as peeqs — and associated rewards that users unlock — into Facebook's News Feed. There, a user's friends can click on the product they peeqed at and begin engaging with relevant products, stores, and boutiques on sneakpeeq as well.

Since layering smart gamification elements into the site, sneakpeeq has seen massive increases in the number of registered, engaged users, and in the valuable behaviors they perform. Here are a few hard numbers:

- A 70 percent month-over-month lift in peeqs
- A 590 percent lift in social shares
- A 935 percent (or 9×) lift in loves
- A 3,000 percent lift in buy clicks
- An 18 percent increase in month-over-month conversions

Expert Witness: Understanding the Community Expert Framework

If the site you seek to gamify is a customer-facing online community, then odds are the community expert framework will meet your needs. It enables you to establish user reputation hierarchies by highlighting reputable contributors. This not only encourages quality contributions, it also helps with content filtering, not to mention enabling site visitors to make user-to-user connections (see Figure 8-4).

Figure 8-4:
The community expert framework is customer-facing and social in nature.

Image courtesy of Badgeville

Recognition of who the user is, what expertise the user carries, and what social standing the user has is important to creating a natural hierarchy within the community. The distinguishing character or personality of an individual is showcased, leading to desirable engagement and increased community participation.

Simply put, the community expert framework is for strengthening and growing diverse communities from fan clubs to Q&A communities. Participants voluntarily pursue expertise in specific topics, unlocking status, prominence, and privilege along the way. Advocates are made of your top users, and the community as a whole benefits from the creation of their celebrity and obsessive engagement.

Status and the rewards or privileges that come with it are valuable to the user because of the sense of worth and pride that comes with an increased standing in a community of peers. When your active community members and top content creators are rewarded with status, their output increases — which helps to improve the overall quality of your site.

Chapter 7 briefly mentioned the reasons the community expert framework works. Here's a recap:

- ✔ **Identity:** Recognizing who users are, what their expertise is, and their social standing creates a hierarchy in the community. Individuals are showcased in the community expert framework, which increases engagement and participation.

- ✔ **Relevance:** Rather than look through pages and pages of content to zero in on answers, the community expert framework showcases users' own expertise. Whatever it is that satisfies a user's needs is easier to find using this framework.

- ✔ **Status:** An individual's relative position when compared to others is key. The rewards and privileges of status enhance an individual's pride in a community of their peers.

Identifying community expert mechanics

The community expert framework could use any number of game mechanics and often does. But in many instances, this framework relies on missions and tracks.

As you've learned, a *mission* requires users to perform a prescribed set of actions, following a guided path of your design. A *track* is simply a collection of missions.

Figure 8-5 shows a site that uses the community expert framework. As you can see, there are multiple users with varying progress along different expertise tracks.

Figure 8-5:
This site shows the community expert framework in action.

Image courtesy of Badgeville

The missions you devise will pertain to topical tasks that enable the user to demonstrate skill or knowledge in a specific area. In effect, missions guide users from novice to expert in a domain.

TIP

It's a good idea to show users where they are in a mission by giving them feedback — for example, displaying a pop-up (see Figure 8-6), when users complete a task or mission. It's also smart to convey to users which tasks they've completed in a mission. A good place to do this is on their profile page or some other easily accessed location (see Figure 8-7).

Figure 8-6:
A pop-up
gives users
crucial
feedback.

Image courtesy of Badgeville

Figure 8-7:
Make it
clear to
users where
they are in a
mission.

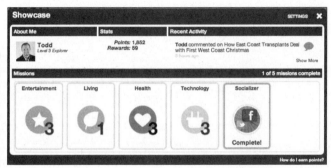

Image courtesy of Badgeville

Exploring popular use cases

As mentioned in Chapter 7, examples of types of businesses that might benefit from the community expert framework include the following:

✔ **Publishing media (blogs, newspapers, and magazines):** Media outlets are places where communities of highly opinionated people converge, ready to debate many different topics. The community expert framework gives those users an opportunity to build a reputation in the topics that interest them most. Users are more likely to leave quality comments when they receive community status for these contributions. This framework integrates seamlessly with common media user experiences such as commenting systems.

✔ **Crowdsourcing (Q&A, creative, and reviews):** Employing crowdsourcing is a little like establishing mini-contests, where the "winner" gets to perform a certain task — such as designing a logo — often for compensation. Crowdsourcing is a great fit for the community expert framework because users are quickly identified for their expertise and social standing.

Often, crowdsourced content has quality issues; it can be difficult to get through all the bad content when you're looking for the diamonds in the rough. Community expert-based reputations help identify and showcase the top content creators.

✔ **Discussion communities and forums:** Traditional Q&A forums, and other online communities less formally, provide a space to ask and answer questions. But this framework provides a meaningful way to improve your users' status and reputations within the community for providing quality answers and contributions, thus improving content and increasing user interconnectivity. The difference is that people build their reputations based on their opinions and interests rather than their concrete expertise.

In Q&A communities, people seek answers — but not all answers are always correct. Reputation systems, coupled with community voting, help identify the top experts in each field — a win-win for both the experts and the askers.

Regardless of use case, the community expert framework is generally best if your site or application is customer-facing and social in nature.

Community expert framework case studies

This section includes case studies that demonstrate the effectiveness of the community expert framework.

Beat the GMAT

Beat the GMAT (BTG) is the world's largest social network for MBA applicants, serving more than 2 million people each year. BTG empowers people to learn, share, teach, and support each other throughout the MBA admissions process.

To generate revenue, Beat the GMAT engages in programs with affiliate GMAT test prep services, such as Kaplan and Princeton Review. As a result, building and harnessing a high-quality community of MBA candidates is a top priority.

To support this business objective, Beat the GMAT recently launched MBA Watch, a social network aimed at MBA applicants, students, admissions officers, GMAT teachers, and MBA consultants. MBA Watch contains a rich set of activities to engage end users. These include commenting on forums, asking questions, or announcing that they were accepted into a specific MBA school.

With the success of the platform relying on key stakeholders contributing content and sharing knowledge, BTG needed to find a dynamic way to engage users and influence key behaviors. Specifically, BTG wanted to do the following:

- ✔ Increase user contributions within education community
- ✔ Drive retention and lifetime value of user base
- ✔ Create an active community of quality MBA applicants

To achieve this, BTG implemented game mechanics on its Beat the GMAT and MBAWatch.com social networking sites, with the main goal of motivating and influencing users to share knowledge about techniques in solving GMAT problems or insights about particular MBA programs.

BTG identified specific behaviors for which to reward users throughout the site. They rendered those rewards as badges on people's profiles. There, other users could see those accomplishments and replicate that same behavior. Examples of badges included the following:

- ✔ **Grammar Champ:** Given to users who write 100 posts in the Sentence Correction forum
- ✔ **Thought Leader:** Awarded to users who collect 250 followers
- ✔ **Problem Solver:** Bestowed on users who write 30 posts in the Problem Solving section

As users were rewarded for these specific actions, their rank and reputation on the site began to rise and be reflected on leaderboards.

Displaying the achievements of prolific users (see Figure 8-8) encourages others to engage in the same desired behavior when they return to the site. On Beat the GMAT, this includes sharing links, reviewing MBA schools, or commenting on specific forums.

Figure 8-8:
Leaderboards like these can help motivate users to engage.

Image courtesy of Beat the GMAT

Check out the results:

- ✔ 195 percent increase in pages visited
- ✔ 370 percent increase on time spent on site
- ✔ 50,000 activities performed by 8,000 users

Interscope Records

Part of Universal Music Group, Interscope Records manages dozens of artists and bands, including LMFAO, Mindless Behavior, and Greyson Chance, as well as American Idol artists Scotty McCreery, Pia Toscano, Hayley Reinhart, and Lauren Alaina.

Interscope's digital team wanted to foster a community of engaged fans across their native fan websites. To achieve this goal, Interscope sought to identify and reward high-value behaviors performed by fans when they visited Interscope's sites — behaviors such as posting, commenting, watching music videos, taking a poll, sharing on social networks, and so on.

Interscope didn't want to host a siloed experience in each separate artist site, though; rather, they wanted a solution that would enable fans to carry their rank and reputation across all the Interscope sites, connect around similar musical tastes, and discover new music.

The solution: Interscope applied gamification to many of its existing websites for both chart-topping and upcoming artists to reward users with badges and achievements tied to specific behaviors and to champion the most engaged fans. Interscope also embedded activity streams on each site that aggregated key behaviors across the whole Interscope network, fostering cross-network participation.

The record company made certain to set up different levels of engagement to mark the progress of their users in completing a set of desired behaviors, including Amateur, New Artist, Gold artist, Platinum Artist, and Diamond artist.

Interscope's gamification program increased the number of active users on Interscope sites, the volume of activities they perform, and overall user retention. Specifically, the results were as follows:

- ✔ 40 percent increase in comments
- ✔ 650 percent increase in engagement
- ✔ 18 percent increase in shares
- ✔ 30 percent more daily comments

Engine Yard

Engine Yard is a leading platform as a service (PaaS) company that provides developers with an easy, cost-effective solution for cloud application development and deployment. Specializing in Ruby on Rails, PHP, and Node.js, the San Francisco-based company serves thousands of customers in 58 countries, ranging from startups to Fortune 500 enterprises. With their extensive tutorials, videos, and podcasts, Engine Yard continually looks for new ways to help developers build and deploy their applications to the cloud.

Engine Yard is passionate about customer service, focusing on innovative ways to a make customers more successful. The Engine Yard support team works 24/7 in IRC and on the phone to make sure customers have everything they need to build and deploy applications that will grow their businesses. With the company's rapid growth, it wanted to build a self-sustaining customer community that would spur innovation, streamline support, capture product feedback, and recognize key contributors in the process.

While Engine Yard leveraged Zendesk to help customers submit support tickets and access the Engine Yard knowledge base, one challenge remained: With busy schedules and many technologies jockeying for their customers' attention, how could they get people to use it?

To address this problem, Engine Yard built game mechanics on top of their Zendesk instance. In just a few short weeks, they had a creative way to engage customers and help them find the information they needed to succeed. Engine Yard designed achievements to reward valuable user behaviors across the community, such as searching their knowledge base. They also created missions — collections of contextually relevant achievements users could earn to unlock special rewards or new ranks or status within the community, such as completing customer surveys.

Specifically, Engine Yard encouraged and rewarded the following behaviors:

- Reading articles
- Searching knowledge base documentation
- Completing customer satisfaction surveys
- Participating in Q&A forums
- Reporting bugs
- Submitting feature requests

As users accumulated rewards, reputation mechanics tracked different levels of engagement tied to expertise. For example, if a user participated extensively in the Ruby section of the community by reading articles or contributing content, she might become a Level 5 Ruby Master.

By driving higher levels of community engagement on their Zendesk instance, Engine Yard is able to better serve customers and help them help themselves. Since deploying gamification in their Zendesk community, Engine Yard has seen the following:

- 20 percent reduction in tickets per customer, on average
- 40 percent increase in forum engagement and knowledge base searches
- A 40 percent improvement in ticket response time by the Engine Yard support team

The Great Pyramid: Exploring the Competitive Pyramid Framework

Does your site already provide a competitive experience? For example, does it host an online or social game? Or maybe a stock-picking challenge? If so, the competitive framework may be just the ticket (see Figure 8-9).

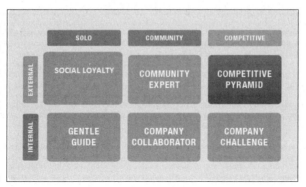

Image courtesy of Badgeville

Figure 8-9:
The competitive pyramid framework is customer-facing and competitive in nature.

The goal of the competitive pyramid framework — which is similar to Xbox Live's popular achievement model (see Figure 8-10) — is to supercharge an already-competitive user experience by tracking player skill levels and presenting challenge opportunities for players to level-up and win.

In essence, you're offering a game within a game, giving players new ways to compete.

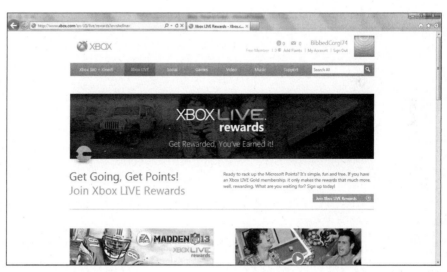

Image courtesy of Xbox Live

Figure 8-10:
The achievement model used on Xbox Live is the inspiration for the competitive pyramid framework.

The competitive pyramid framework also works well for sites that involve prediction — think stock prediction, sports prediction (such as Fantasy Football), gambling, and the like.

So, what's with the pyramid analogy? Think of it like this: At the pinnacle of the pyramid is whoever has the most points on the site. One level down is the player with the most points in a particular category. The base of the pyramid is where players demonstrate mastery of individual skills.

For example, consider a poker site. At the top of the pyramid will be the player with the most points overall. The middle level might be the top player in Five-Card Stud (as opposed to, say, the top Texas Hold 'Em player). And the bottom level would display the specific accomplishments, like winning a certain number of hands with bluffs or going all-in and winning.

In that example, players might earn achievements by, say, hitting a flush in spades or four kings. Even if someone isn't terribly good at Five-Card Stud, he might still do well on the achievement front — thereby increasing his engagement in the game (see Figure 8-11).

Figure 8-11:
An example of a competitive pyramid.

Top player on the site

Top five-card stud player

Top achievement earner

A five-card stud competitve pyramid

Illustration by Wiley, Composition Services Graphics

The competitive pyramid framework is effective only in competitive environments. Most typical sites are not a good fit.

Here are some of the mechanisms that make the competitive pyramid framework work:

- **Competition:** Users in a game environment naturally enjoy winning. Given more opportunities to compete, players meet the challenge in a variety of competitions.

- **Specialization:** Specific expertise enables a user to focus his efforts on winning against a broad base of competition. Winning creates a desire for more victory and leads players to grow into other specializations, in a cycle of winning and engagement.

✔ **Challenges:** Adding game layers to an experience, with chances to level-up, motivates players. Multiple game layers maintains user interest and involvement.

Identifying competitive pyramid mechanics

The competitive pyramid is great for customer-facing, competitive sites (such as game sites), but it isn't appropriate for sites without competitive game-like content.

It can rely on a number of game mechanics, but focuses on the following:

✔ **The use of rewards for the completion of small challenges:** In addition to earning regular "in-game" points, users under the competitive pyramid are rewarded for completing certain achievements — for example, hitting four of a kind on a poker site.

✔ **Missions for larger challenges:** As mentioned, it's a good idea to show users where they are in a mission by giving them feedback — for example, displaying pop-up notifications when users complete a task or mission. It's also smart to convey to users which tasks they've completed in a mission as well as which ones they have yet to finish in order to complete the mission.

✔ **Leaderboards or levels, to denote mastery:** Again, in the competitive pyramid framework, leaderboards are presented in a pyramid fashion, with top users site-wide at the top, top users in a given category in the middle, and top achievement earners (the ones who've completed small challenges) at the base.

Exploring popular use cases

As mentioned in Chapter 7, examples of types of sites that might benefit from the pyramid challenge framework include the following:

✔ **Test and quiz sites:** For communities that offer tests and quizzes in a competitive environment, the competitive pyramid framework supports a larger game connecting smaller performance wins on each individual test.

✔ **Prediction communities:** In prediction communities, the competitive pyramid framework offers a powerful way to compare success across a wide variety of measurements. This framework enables users to compare points across categories and surface the most accurate participants.

✔ **Games and social gaming:** In existing gaming communities, the competitive pyramid framework offers an Xbox Live type of achievement, creating additional challenges across your community to guide ongoing participation.

The competitive pyramid framework is generally best if your site or application is customer-facing and competitive in nature.

Competitive pyramid example

This example considers a website that deals in fictional sales of celebrity "stocks." The value of a stock is based on the career income of the star in question and is measured in fictional H bucks. The content of the site, which is highly social, is effectively a big game containing a great degree of natural competition with multiple areas of content (music stars, movie/TV stars, athletes) — perfect for the competitive pyramid framework (see Figure 8-12).

Figure 8-12:
An example of a site using the competitive framework.

Image courtesy of Badgeville

Behaviors

The primary behaviors on this example site are buying and selling stocks. The increase and decrease in stock values could also be considered behaviors (although they're not directly performed by the users). For example, if a player earns H5,000, this could be logged as a behavior: "End the day up H5,000."

Achievements

Achievements are subdivided by category, with category representing a single mission. The broad categories are along genre lines:

- Actors
- Athletes
- Musicians
- Politicians

Specific achievements are category-specific and include things like the following:

- Earn more than 5 percent in a single day on a celebrity
- Earn more than 10 percent in a single day on a celebrity
- Buy an IPO (newly added celebrity)
- Short a celebrity
- Receive five likes on a single forum post stock tip

From a framing perspective, achievements should demonstrate mastery. That is, they should be an identity metric of sorts. Earning H is already a measure of mastery; the real opportunity with achievements is to surface specific accomplishments — and the more creativity and depth put into designing achievements, the better.

Simple achievements like buying an IPO can also encourage users to engage in activities in which they might not naturally engage.

Points

The site already contains a points system: H. In addition, players receive separate points, called R (reputation points), for various achievements. Achievements pay out both H and R to help incentivize achievements and establish a clear new dimension of competition (category-specific reputation).

Having two types of points lets you reward repeated achievements with one currency (H) but not the other (R). Players have an overall total H and R. In addition, within each category, players have subtotal H and R scores.

Within each mission category, achievements aren't ordered. Therefore, all achievements should have assigned points values that are scored against a universal standard of difficulty. Simple tasks like buying an IPO should be worth few points. More advanced, skill-based tasks — like earning more than 10 percent in a single day on a celebrity — should be worth more.

Splitting achievements into categories causes reputation scores to become areas of expertise or social identifiers. Achievements should be designed to range from very easy to very difficult. Only a small percentage of users should be able to get every achievement in a category, and only a handful of your top super users should be able to get every achievement in every category.

Decay

Decay is difficult to capture in the competitive pyramid model, but it's usually not necessary. After all, a natural degree of decay exists in the underlying site: If you don't show up to compete, you miss out on opportunities to buy better celebrities and fall behind on the leaderboards.

Chapter 9

Employee-Facing Frameworks

· ·

In This Chapter

▶ Reviewing the gentle guide framework

▶ Contemplating the company collaborator framework

▶ Checking out the company challenge framework

· ·

As Chapter 7 mentions, three of the six frameworks are internal, or geared toward employee-facing experiences.

This chapter explores these three frameworks in greater detail:

✔ The gentle guide framework

✔ The company collaborator framework

✔ The company challenge framework

Gentle Giant: Exploring the Gentle Guide Framework

Gentle guide is a hand-holding, employee-facing framework, designed to help employees complete a process of steps — be they everyday job tasks or a specific, process-oriented training program for required certifications (see Figure 9-1).

Figure 9-1:
The gentle guide frame-work is an employee-facing, solo framework.

Image courtesy of Badgeville

The gentle guide framework helps keep employees task-oriented by assigning them a mission of objectives and rewarding them for completing required activities on time. Gentle guide is all about setting a routine and repeating it. It's used to help keep simple tasks on the forefront of an employee's mind.

Often, the gentle guide framework is integrated into existing task-manage-ment or performance-incentive programs. A significant advantage of using gentle guide over pre-existing performance incentive programs, however, is its ability to track and reward a wide range of behaviors.

In the modern business world, the difference between a top performer and an average performer is increasingly subtle and difficult to track offline. You can apply the gentle guide framework for floor workers such as salesmen, cus-tomer service specialists, technicians, and so on, up to branch and regional managers.

When it's really firing on all cylinders, the gentle guide framework can reduce the overhead of managing employees, particularly in large organizations. Even the most complex jobs are made manageable with focused, step-by-step rewards.

As Chapter 7 previews, here are some of the mechanisms that guide the gentle guide framework:

- ✔ **Baby steps:** Gentle guide breaks big tasks into smaller, easily accom-plished micro-tasks. Each micro-task then becomes a little victory, and the larger task isn't so scary.

- ✔ **Visualization of progress:** Through points, checklists, and badges, users know when they've performed desirable behaviors. Visualizing their progress is key to keeping them performing.

> ✔ **Positive reinforcement:** Positive reinforcement leads to lasting behavioral modification. Users are motivated to continue performing towards their goals while accomplishing tasks and receiving recognition.

Identifying gentle guide mechanics

The gentle guide framework relies strongly on missions and tracks — but with a twist: The missions and tracks are essentially task lists. As missions and tracks are completed, users earn points and rewards.

To refresh your memory, a *mission* (also sometimes called a *challenge* or *quest*) requires users to perform a prescribed set of actions. Sometimes, these actions must occur in a certain order. Missions of this type are called *progression missions*. Other times, actions can occur in any order. These missions are called *random missions*.

A *track* is simply a series of missions. Much like progressive or random missions, you can define a track as being ordered or unordered. An *ordered* track means you must complete the missions in the order they appear in the track. An *unordered* track means you can complete the missions in any order.

With the gentle guide framework, missions, tracks, and rewards must be repeatable and are typically reset on a daily or weekly basis.

Note that with gentle guide, you can specify a time interval for a track. For example, you might set the time interval for a track to be a week. You use intervals when the player is expected to perform the tasks repeatedly within a recurring time period — such as a day, week, month, or quarter.

Employing progress bars is a good idea with the gentle guide framework. This way, users know exactly how far along they are in their mission.

Exploring popular use cases

Unlike some of the other frameworks, the gentle guide framework doesn't necessarily lend itself to use within particular industries. Rather, gentle guide can work in any industry with certain jobs that involve performing a specific set of repetitive tasks on a regular basis — daily, weekly, monthly, quarterly, or what have you.

Gentle guide also works well for more creative tasks; the goals are just more open-ended.

TIP

In a nutshell, gentle guide is all about performance management, regardless of industry.

Often, gentle guide is used in environments where employees aren't knowledge workers — for example, in service and manufacturing.

Suppose you manage a frozen yogurt store called Pink Tangerine. You might use gentle guide to help keep your employees on track during their shifts. Their mission might include such tasks as keeping the yogurt machines full, replenishing the spoon and napkin holders, counting the cash drawer, and so forth (see Figure 9-2).

By completing the mission during each shift, employees earn points. Then, the next time they work, the mission begins again. This helps ensure that they stay on track and at the same time enables you, the store manager, to track monthly progress — meaning higher-level goals could also be reached. You could then use monthly performance as the trigger for rewards such as bonuses, recognition, and so forth.

Or maybe you're in sales. In that case, your mission might involve quarterly sales-related tasks — cold-calling potential clients, visiting customers, closing deals, and so on. If you complete all the tasks in the mission within the time frame, you'll be duly rewarded; once the quarter is complete, the mission will reset.

Figure 9-2:
The gentle guide framework is perfect for a scenario like this one.

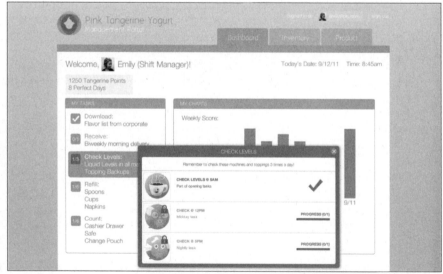

Image courtesy of Badgeville

Note that in this scenario, behaviors could also have a qualitative aspect. For example, deal size might be a factor. Indeed, it's this very combination of qualitative and quantitative that makes gamification so powerful.

Another example might involve the completion of certain compliance-related tasks, such as an annual review of safety procedures. In that case, you could set up a single ordered track called Yearly Safety Training, with various missions — for example, Fire Safety and Air Safety. Both missions would require employees to watch a video and complete a drill in the allotted time period (one year, for example).

You could use a progress bar to indicate how much of the mission is complete (see Figure 9-3).

Figure 9-3: The review of safety procedures might be a good fit for gentle guide.

Image courtesy of Badgeville

Finally, gentle guide may be the best framework for *onboarding* — the process by which new employees obtain the knowledge, skills, and behaviors necessary to become effective members of an organization.

The fact is, many new employees fail to leverage the tools available to them during their first few weeks of employment at an organization. By using gentle guide, employers can give new employees a mission containing a list of tasks to complete. Typical tasks might include the following:

- Filling out insurance forms
- Meeting team members
- Logging in to the company intranet
- Interacting on the employee social network
- Watching video tutorials
- Reading the employee handbook

Customer-facing use cases

Although the gentle guide framework is typically used in enterprise settings, there are some consumer uses for it. A great example is medical adherence — that is, helping people remember to take medications. For many, this is a behavior that must occur multiple times per day, every day.

The gentle guide framework is also a great choice if your customer-facing site or app is about encouraging healthy behaviors such as logging exercises and daily nutrition. It also works well in training scenarios — for example, achieving certification or learning a language — in which setting a schedule is key.

There could also be customer-facing variations of the onboarding use case — a sort of *tour guide* version. For example, suppose you run a subscription-based site, and your goal is to persuade free users to upgrade to paid accounts. You might devise a mission that involves a series of tasks designed to encourage the user to explore your site in its entirety within a certain time frame. This variation would not be repetitive, but otherwise many of the standard gentle guide mechanics would apply.

However, unlike with other gentle guide use cases, this mission is not repeated.

Essentially, you're giving new employees a standardized checklist that is both engaging and informative and that gently nudges them when they forget about it in the hustle and bustle of a new job.

Gentle guide example: Safety and efficiency

Suppose you're a cog-producing facility that wants to reduce the number of work-related injuries and increase employee efficiency. In that case, you might use the gentle guide framework to set up missions that reward the following repetitive behaviors:

- ✔ Clocking in: 5 points
- ✔ Refilling the metal slugs bin at 11 a.m.: 10 points
- ✔ Clocking out at lunch time: 5 points
- ✔ Clocking in when lunch ends: 5 points
- ✔ Refilling metal slugs bin at 3 p.m.: 10 points
- ✔ Checking fluid levels in the cog grinder: 10 points
- ✔ Clocking out: 5 points

Do a little math, and you'll notice that employees can earn a perfect daily score of 50 points. On top of that, you might also define some bonus-point opportunities:

- ✔ Reporting another employee for not using handrails while crossing over the cog grinder: 20 points
- ✔ Finishing a day with no rejected cogs: 10 points
- ✔ Finish a day with 400+ cogs punched: 10 points

To make things more interesting, you could give every employee who scores 250 points or more in a week a special reward — say, a $50 bonus or a gift card to a local restaurant. Employees scoring 300 or more might be entitled to something even sweeter — maybe $100 or lunch with the CEO.

In Good Company: Understanding the Company Collaborator Framework

Suppose you work at MegaHugeGigantor Co., Inc. It is, as its name implies, an enormous company. As you might expect, in a company this large, connecting people who have questions with people who have answers can be an ordeal.

Enter the company collaborator framework (see Figure 9-4). This framework is often employed in forum settings, but can also be used alongside other social software tools, such as Microsoft's Yammer, Salesforce.com's Chatter, Jive, and Lithium. It's used internally within organizations to help connect people who have problems with people who have solutions. With company collaborator, employees in need can locate experts who have the knowledge to help.

Figure 9-4:
The company collaborator framework is an employee-facing, social framework.

Image courtesy of Badgeville

Company collaborator is similar to the community expert framework. As you can see in Chapter 8, community expert enables sites to establish user-reputation hierarchies by rewarding and highlighting reputable contributors. What's the difference? With the company collaborator framework, that reputation is built on professional knowledge and shared within an organization rather than with the Web at large. Indeed, this reputation becomes an integral piece of an employee's identity.

Another difference between community expert and company collaborator is that a company collaborator system needs to take into account existing reputation models, such as job title, seniority, and so on.

Company collaborator is also similar to gentle guide in that it is employee-facing, but it's for a different type of employee. That is, if gentle guide is for soldiers, company collaborator is for artists — think engineers, designers, strategists, or any employee who relies on creativity and communication to excel.

Company collaborator sets out to establish a reputational bond between employees and the organization. Top performers are recognized for their status and problems are matched with solutions.

Here are a few of the mechanisms employed by company collaborator:

- **Identity:** Recognizing who users are, what expertise they have, and their social status helps create natural roles in the community. Playing up the value of individuals is a good way to enhance workplace participation.

- **Relevance:** Stop paging through old manuals or asking people in the nearest cubes how to do stuff — company collaborator sorts out all the expertise in the company, making it easy and quick to find who knows what you need to know. That boosts productivity and cuts down on incorrect information.

- **Status:** Everyone wants to be awarded the proper status based on what they know best. When they get that status, they feel a sense of worth, pride, and job satisfaction.

Identifying company collaborator mechanics

Given that the company collaborator framework is so similar to the community expert model, it makes sense that both rely heavily on missions and tracks (although just about any mechanic can be used). And as with community expert, conveying the reputation of site users is critical. In fact, this conveying of reputation is the linchpin of the company collaborator framework.

Relieving employee pain points

Many organizations say they want to be more collaborative. But many fail to say *why*. When it comes to collaboration, pinpointing your real goal is critical. And the goal should be one that will help relieve a pain point for your employees.

For example, say your sales team constantly emails your product people with questions — which is frustrating because the product team maintains a product wiki that contains a lot of the answers. That's a pain point for product

people. Your goal, then, might be for the sales team to read the wiki. You also want the product team to continue to maintain the wiki, adding new information as needed.

You could easily use the company collaborator framework to encourage both of those behaviors. Not only would members of both teams receive rewards for completing relevant missions, but their business processes would improve.

The trick with collaboration in general is motivating users to participate in the first place. Indeed there is often natural inhibition to participation. One inhibitor is that employees may be hesitant to share their knowledge — much as a chef might resist sharing the recipe for his signature dish. You're sometimes talking about job security, after all. Another may be that people are satisfied with the tools already at their disposal — and may be a little anxious that the big cheeses in corporate will be able to see everything they write on the forum, for example. As a result, a cultural shift is often in order.

That's where rewards come in. By rewarding users for performing the most valuable behaviors — for example, asking a question or answering one (perhaps more than once) — you can begin to effect that change. After all, there's a big perceptual difference between always answering the same question (annoying) and answering the same question to level-up your status to JavaScript Expert!

 As you implement the company collaborator framework, it's a good idea to position key employees to amp up their sharing of information. Inevitably, more employees will jump on board as they realize how effective the forum is for obtaining the answers they need. Getting managers involved — not just the CEO, but your day-to-day managers who have regular contact with the rank and file — is also key, as a trickle-down effect will almost certainly occur. In the end, as more users have the opportunity to showcase their value, improve their status within the company, and find the information they need more easily, increased community participation will occur.

Exploring popular use cases

Similar to the gentle guide framework, the company collaborator framework doesn't really lend itself to one industry over another. Rather, company collaborator is geared for organizations of a certain size: big ones with lots of employees, possibly in far-flung locations (see Figure 9-5).

Specifically, the framework is most often used in internal corporate communities, especially those with established community forums, where it can help employees make more efficient and meaningful connections. It's also used in developer and partner communities.

Internal wikis can also benefit from the use of the company collaborator framework to highlight employees who share the most useful content.

Figure 9-5: Corporate communities are an ideal host for the company collaborator framework.

Image courtesy of Badgeville

The point is, it's usually not enough to simply offer community tools to your employees and expect them to use them. Sure, some might at first, just because the tools are like shiny new toys. But there's a risk of that behavior dying off.

You'll likely have to incentivize employees to help them become more collaborative. For example, you might offer special rewards to early adopters. That's where gamification — specifically, the company collaborator framework — comes in. Having this layer of incentivization clearly drives participation, especially when employees feel like collaboration is just one more thing to do on top of everything else that's expected of them.

Company collaborator example: Improving retention, productivity, and knowledge sharing

Imagine you work for a software company that wants to improve retention of top performers, increase productivity of junior programmers, and improve communication and knowledge sharing across departments. In that case, you could use the company collaborator framework to reward in five expertise-based categories, or tracks:

- ✔ The coding language
- ✔ The scripting library
- ✔ The company database
- ✔ The product
- ✔ Miscellaneous

Employees could post and answer questions in these five categories in the company's internal knowledge base. The person who asks a question can then flag certain responses as helpful. Those who answer questions progress through the expertise levels of the various tracks based on the number of helpful votes they receive in the corresponding topics, leveling up as follows:

- ✔ Level 1: 1 helpful vote
- ✔ Level 2: 5 helpful votes
- ✔ Level 3: 10 helpful votes
- ✔ Level 4: 25 helpful votes
- ✔ Level 5: 50 helpful votes
- ✔ Level 6: 75 helpful votes
- ✔ Level 7: 125 helpful votes

To make things even more interesting, any questions that are left unresolved (not closed by at least one vote) for more than three days could be escalated to "Genius" level. The first person to receive a helpful vote on a Genius level question earns a Genius point. An employee's identification in the system could then consist of his or her name, a photo, five track-rank icons, and a Genius score.

Deloitte: Company collaborator framework case study

With nearly 200,000 consultants spread globally, Deloitte is the largest consulting firm on the planet. Focusing on audits, financial advisory, tax, and consulting, Deloitte employees have vast expertise in avariety of industries.

With the sheer size of the company came the challenge of knowledge silos. A *knowledge silo* is typically a person or department that has gathered a significant amount of knowledge, but for whatever reason, fails to share it with the rest of the organization. For example, one consultant working with a consumer goods company in the United States might miss out on some valuable information learned by a colleague in Australia, causing redundant work and slowing the time to serve clients.

To address this problem, Deloitte added Yammer, the enterprise social network. Yammer's a bit like Facebook, but it's designed for use within a company. Its chief aim is to improve communication and collaboration. One major hurdle remained: influencing the behavior of thousands of consultants to adopt social software after years of being conditioned to e-mail and other similar technologies.

To motivate employees to share valuable knowledge, Deloitte created an internal Who What Where mobile app that rewards consultants who "check in" and share who they're meeting with on the road, what they discussed, and where it took place.

As employees gain rewards such as badges for sharing this valuable information with their colleagues, those rewards are broadcast into the Deloitte Yammer Activity Stream. This enables employees who unlock badges and rewards to showcase their status, reputation, and expertise — even to executives at Deloitte, who also engage with Yammer (including Deloitte's CEO). Employees can also view their accomplishments in their profile.

The results? Check it out:

- Increased knowledge sharing
- Improved expertise location among consultants globally
- Better alignment between the company and its employees
- Reduced turnover

Challenge Response: Exploring the Company Challenge Framework

The company challenge framework is an employee-facing model that's designed to increase productivity through friendly competition. This framework adds a layer of competition to the gentle guide framework, which focuses on repetitive or prescriptive tasks — mopping floors, entering data, and the like (see Figure 9-6).

Figure 9-6:
The company challenge framework is an employee-facing, competitive framework.

Image courtesy of Badgeville

This layer of competition takes the form of teams, allowing different groups within the organization to compete against each other.

With company challenge, the daily grind becomes a game played across departments and locations. This competition not only motivates employees and increases productivity, but it makes work more fun than Joan Rivers at a theme park.

Teams compete for accuracy, efficiency, and thoroughness. Leaderboards, standings, and comparisons bring out the competitive spirit and improve teamwork. Teams diffuse the individual pressures associated with competition.

As mentioned in Chapter 7, here are some of the reasons company challenge is effective:

✓ **Visualizing progress:** Levels, points, leaderboards, achievements, and badges provide users with feedback on where they are and how to level-up. The visual aspect is key to keeping employees performing.

✔ **Rewards:** Team and individual rewards can set employee behaviors.

✔ **Teamwork:** When teams win, players feel the victory, but team defeat doesn't hurt as badly as individual defeat. Loss is spread out over the team.

Identifying company challenge mechanics

Like the gentle guide framework, this framework relies heavily on task-based missions and tracks, which help keep employees focused and on target during their work.

The gentle guide section earlier cites an example of a yogurt store called Pink Tangerine. Employees in that store might, as part of their daily mission, complete such tasks as keeping the yogurt machines full, replenishing the spoon and napkin holders, counting the cash drawer, and so on. By completing the mission during each shift, employees earn points and rewards. Then, the next time they work, the mission begins again.

The company challenge framework expands on this idea by dividing employees into teams. Suddenly, employees are no longer simply completing their work for rewards; they're playing a game against each other. Now it's the morning shift in this Pink Tangerine yogurt shop against the evening shift. Or it could be this Pink Tangerine outlet against the one across town, or against all the Pink Tangerines in the region — or even all the Pink Tangerines in the nation.

Teams are a most excellent mechanic. They almost never go wrong.

As with other frameworks, clearly measured metrics — that is, points, leaderboards (both team and individual), levels, and so on — provide actionable feedback. Through these metrics, employees know what they've achieved. This visualization of status is instrumental in keeping employees performing at their peak. And of course rewards are important, whether driven by monetary incentives, privileges, or recognition. You can issue rewards on both an individual basis and a team basis.

Exploring popular use cases

The company challenge framework doesn't really lend itself to use in one industry more than another. Rather, company challenge is geared for organizations that want to improve productivity — especially for employees whose tasks are somewhat repetitive or prescriptive. We mentioned the yogurt shop example. Another one might be a grocery store (see Figure 9-7).

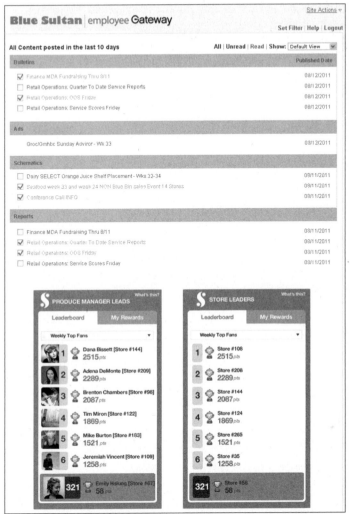

Figure 9-7:
The company challenge framework is perfect for a scenario like this one.

Here are a few more examples of areas in which company challenge might work well:

✔ **Sales productivity:** You could increase sales productivity by adding the company challenge framework to your CRM systems. This framework allows you to create an additional layer of competition for sales and marketing team members. As members of your sales team compete, their efficiency and revenues will likely increase.

- **Team performance management:** The company challenge framework is ideal in large corporations where teams have specific metrics against which their success is measured. In these settings, this framework effectively increases productivity and promotes corporate-wide teamwork with friendly competition.

- **Support/call center operations:** This framework works well in support and help-desk systems. In these cases, you might create a layer of competition for support ticketing systems, with employees and teams who successfully close the most tickets declared the winners.

- **Human resources:** In this case, you might gamify the process of hiring employees, with the team that hires the most qualified candidates in a quarter being recognized.

- **Claims processing:** Consider a company that processes insurance claims. Teams that process the most claims in a quarter might receive a financial bonus or some free stuff.

- **Nonprofit:** Suppose you're trying to get people to raise money for a certain cause. You can organize them into teams and reward them for performing such key tasks as making calls, sending letters, or raising the most money.

Really, any organization whose employees are already arranged in teams with specific metrics that measure their success is an excellent candidate for the company challenge framework. In these settings, this framework effectively increases productivity and promotes company-wide teamwork with friendly competition.

Company challenge example: Reducing injuries

Consider a gear-producing factory mentioned earlier in this chapter, in the discussion of the gentle guide framework. The company wants to reduce the number of work-related injuries and increase employee efficiency across the whole corporation.

As you may recall, the company develops the following reward program:

- Clocking in: 5 points

- Refilling metal slugs bin at 11 a.m.: 10 points

- Clocking out at lunchtime: 5 points

- Clocking in when lunch ends: 5 points

- ✔ Refilling metal slugs bin at 3 p.m.: 10 points
- ✔ Checking fluid levels in gear grinder: 10 points
- ✔ Clocking out: 5 points

Note that employees can earn a perfect daily score of 50 points. On top of that, you might also define some bonus-point opportunities:

- ✔ Reporting another employee for not using handrails while crossing over the gear grinder: 20 points
- ✔ Finishing a day with no rejected gears: 10 points
- ✔ Finishing a day with more than 400 gears punched: 10 points

In this example, however, the program also includes two leaderboards:

- ✔ **Location-based competition board:** This board ranks all the gear jockeys in a factory. Each factory has its own local competition board.
- ✔ **Company-wide competition board:** This board ranks the three factories by the total score of all employees in each factory. (Scores may need to be adapted in some way to accommodate unequal numbers of employees. Otherwise, sites with more employees might naturally incur more points, giving them an unfair advantage over sites with fewer employees.)

Both boards reset monthly. At the end of each month, the leading factory is awarded with a paid half-day, and the leading scorer at that factory is awarded with a paid full-day.

Part III
Getting Your Gamification Program Off the Ground

The 5th Wave   By Rich Tennant

"It's so easy to introduce fresh incentives using our gamification program. I just wish I didn't have to let the customers win them."

In this part . . .

In this part, you'll get the 411 on whether to build your own gamification program from scratch or partner with a provider. You'll also get solid info on which providers are out there, at the ready. Next, you'll discover exactly who belongs on your gamification team, as well as the basics of configuring and deploying your program. And the chapter on analytics gives you the mere tip of the iceberg in terms of what kind of data you can gather with gamification. Finally, you'll get a glimpse of just where gamification may be heading in the future.

Chapter 10

Choosing a Gamification Provider

In This Chapter

▶ The pros and cons of buying versus building

▶ Exploring gamification providers

▶ Accessing open-source resources

*N*ow that you understand what gamification can do for your organization and have a basic idea what type of program and framework would be best suited for your business objectives, you're (hopefully) thinking, "Where do I sign up?"

Hold up. Before you can begin the process of implementing a gamification program, you have to make a few key decisions. First, you need to decide whether to build a system from the ground up using whoever you have on hand in-house — or to partner with a gamification provider. If you opt for the latter, you'll need to get an idea of what providers are out there. This chapter is here to help you get started.

Decisions, Decisions: Deciding Whether to Build or Buy

To be or not to be — yeah, that's one question. Here's another one: Build or buy? That is, should you attempt to build your gamification program in house from the ground up? Or should you buy a gamification system from a company that specializes in that sort of thing?

Disclosure alert: One of the authors of this book is the CEO of Badgeville, a major gamification provider. That means he has some strong opinions on the *build or buy* conundrum, most of which lean toward *buy*.

If the gamification program you envision is dead simple — that is, if the system you use to weigh behaviors and rewards is never ever in a million kajillion years going to change, and if you're not too worried about anti-gaming mechanics — then you could probably build your own gamification program. If you're on a budget, then this route will probably seem even more attractive, given that most gamification providers do not operate as charities.

But often, when people attempt to build a gamification program in house, even one they think is very simple, they soon discover that what looks simple is in fact quite complex. As but one example, take the code used to create a simple rule that assigns a reward to a particular behavior. Hand-coding that kind of thing is a lot harder than simply selecting a reward and a corresponding behavior from a graphical user interface (GUI) — which you can do using platforms offered by many third-party gamification providers (see Figure 10-1).

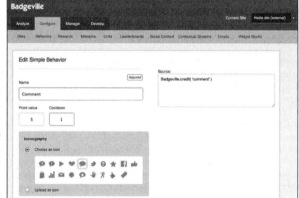

Figure 10-1: Using a GUI is *waaaaay* easier than coding stuff by hand.

Image courtesy of Badgeville

Now extrapolate. You wouldn't have to just code that one behavior and reward; you'd have to code *everything* — leaderboards, teams, missions, time frames, meta data, and so on. And every time you discovered you needed to make a change, you'd have to code that, too. In time, your fingers could fall off from all that typing, which would be unfortunate.

If you do opt to build your own gamification program, there are open-source gamification tools available for the taking. These can help ease the pain of coding all those behaviors and rewards. You'll learn about these tools later in this chapter.

Opting to partner with a gamification provider isn't just easier and finger-saving, however. The best providers offer a platform with tools that enable you to devise a more robust gamification program — one that helps you not only to drive valuable user behavior, but collect and analyze data about those behaviors through the use of analytics. (You'll find out all about analytics in Chapter 13.) Some gamification providers even have tools that enable you to port all your data to a CSV file and copy it to other systems, all with the click of a button! (A CSV file — short for *comma separated value* — is a common, relatively simple file format supported by loads of consumer, business, and scientific applications. It's often used to move data between programs that natively operate on incompatible formats.)

Speaking of platforms: Not only do provider's platforms offer tools that enable you to devise a robust gamification program, many of those platforms are also agnostic from a technology standpoint. So, suppose you want to gamify a forum on your site. Regardless of what type of software your forum runs on — say, Jive or Lithium (or whatever) — the gamification platform will work.

Here are a few other reasons going with a gamification provider is the recommended route:

- ✔ Will your organization be able to handle the spike in traffic that inevitably occurs with a successful gamification program? A solid gamification provider will handle the processing of all the behaviors being performed and rewarded on *its* end, freeing your computing and network resources for other mission-critical tasks.

- ✔ You need a gamification program that gives you room to grow. As soon as your program gets bigger, you need it to scale. Odds are, if you try the DIY route, it won't scale.

   Many organizations have tried to build their own gamification systems, only to discover that what they've developed is too rigid. It doesn't allow for the easy addition of new features over time. Without that ability, you'll quickly find that the system you built becomes out of date very quickly.

- ✔ Sure, what you're rewarding today might make sense. But as any organization that sold VHS tapes can tell you, business moves fast. What if tomorrow you realize that giving more points to users who write reviews will help you meet a key new business objective? You'll need a way to do that quickly and easily. Building a system that allows for that is no small task.

   Ideally, you're going to learn a lot as you implement your gamification program. After all, gamification has everything to do with behavior and psychology — and what we know about that changes all the time. Plus, what people do or want to do will likely evolve. All that means you must be adaptable. Avoid building something too simple or too short-sighted.

✔ When you introduce a new feature to your gamification program, you can't just crank it out and slap it up on your site. Every time a gamification provider comes up with a new feature, they have to develop it, test it, document it, and so on. It's not a matter of merely writing the code; it's about owning it — and it involves a significant cost. Why not let a provider deal with all that rather than trying to tackle it yourself?

✔ Gamification providers strive to constantly improve their platform. Indeed, it's amazing how quickly they can iterate on ideas and make them useful. Then again, it's their full-time job and area of expertise — they've already found ten ways around a problem that you'll discover tomorrow and which will vex you for weeks. They have all these skills they can leverage within. No offense, but that probably won't be the case in your own organization.

✔ A good gamification provider offers more than just tools; the best ones also offer advice on designing and implementing your gamification program. This expertise can significantly shorten the time you need to get your program up and running. It can also improve the programs itself, making it smoother and more authentic feeling to the user. Remember: The best gamification programs are barely noticeable. They seem organic.

That said, there may be cases where building your own program is the way to go. Maybe it's very simple, or you already have the core competency in house, or you have serious budget constraints. Nevertheless, partnering with a provider is almost always the better choice.

A gamification that's half-assed (pardon our French) is worse than no gamification program at all. You're either serious about gamification or you're not. If you're not serious about it, you probably shouldn't do it.

So, to recap, here are a few key reasons to buy rather than build:

✔ Hidden rules complexity

✔ Sophisticated GUI that enables easy configuration and reconfiguration

✔ Refined, optimized architecture

✔ Team of experts

✔ Analytics

✔ Processing power

✔ Flexibility

✔ Scalability

Buying: Identifying Gamification Providers

If you've opted to go the provider route, the next obvious question is, what provider should you choose? Although gamification is a relatively new industry, there are numerous organizations to choose from. Here are just a few:

- ✔ 500Friends
- ✔ Badgeville
- ✔ Big Door
- ✔ Bunchball
- ✔ CrowdTwist
- ✔ Gigya
- ✔ IActionable
- ✔ Seriosity

This is by no means an exhaustive list of gamification providers. It's a growing industry, and new players emerge (and old ones fold) at a breathtaking pace.

500Friends

500Friends (www.500friends.com; see Figure 10-2) butters its bread by, as co-founder and CEO Justin Yoshimura says, "helping to level the playing field and give retailers, regardless of size, the ability to deploy rich and responsive programs that extend their relationships beyond the purchase and turn customers into advocates." How? By enabling retailers to create and deploy a compelling customer experience that recognizes and rewards actions directly tied to their marketing objectives. The results are twofold: higher search-engine rankings and acquisition of new customers by word-of-mouth. 500Friends now boasts more than 40 top retailers on its platform, including Internet Retailer Top 100 companies such as Shoebuy, US Autoparts, and Build.com.

Figure 10-2:
500Friends
focuses on
the retail
sector.

Image courtesy of 500Friends

Badgeville

An industry leader, Badgeville (www.badgeville.com; see Figure 10-3) offers services for gamification, reputation management, and social mechanics, drawing on techniques from social gaming, traditional loyalty programs, and social networking to influence users to perform high-value behavior. Cloud connectors and ISV programs allow for easy integration of the Badgeville system into dozens of the world's top enterprise and social applications. Badgeville has laid claim to more than 200 customers spanning virtually every industry, including Oracle, EMC, Samsung, NBC, Deloitte, Rogers Communications, Bell Media, CA Technologies, The Active Network, Appirio, Recyclebank, eBay, and many more. Badgeville boasts the most experience in the industry and, with $40 million raised in venture capital, is the most funded company in gamification.

Just a reminder that one of the authors of this book is the CEO of Badgeville. Note, too, that the frameworks discussed in the chapters in Part II are rooted in Badgeville's research, experience, and product offerings.

Figure 10-3:
Badgeville is all about gamification, reputation management, and social mechanics.

Image courtesy of Badgeville

Big Door

Founded in 2009, Seattle-based Big Door (www.bigdoor.com; see Figure 10-4) aims to help Web publishers, marketers, and developers grow and engage their communities. Using its gamified loyalty platform, customers — who range from small, independent bloggers to Dell, Major League Baseball, and Nickelodeon — can quickly build game mechanics into their online experiences and applications. Innovative user incentives —including sharing; the ability to earn virtual currency, rewards, points, and badges; and participation in quests — achieve deeper brand affinity.

Figure 10-4: Big Door uses game mechanics to promote deeper brand affinity.

Image courtesy of Big Door

Bunchball

Founded in 2005, Bunchball (www.bunchball.com) boasts a healthy roster of customers, including Warner Bros., Comcast, NBC Universal, Stella & Dot, Chiquita, Playboy, Bravo, The USA Network, and LiveOps use Bunchball's Nitro gamification platform. Nitro includes powerful analytics to create customized, actionable, and scalable user experiences for consumers, employees, and partners.

CrowdTwist

The mission of CrowdTwist (www.crowdtwist.com; see Figure 10-5) is to enable organizations to reward points to users for their engagement, social influence, and spending. CrowdTwist focuses on issuing monetary rewards rather than virtual ones. That is, rather than being badge-centric, they issue rewards like one-of-a-kind experiences, branded merchandise, exclusive items, partner-sponsored rewards, deals, and discounts. Advanced analytics and management and reporting tools are also available.

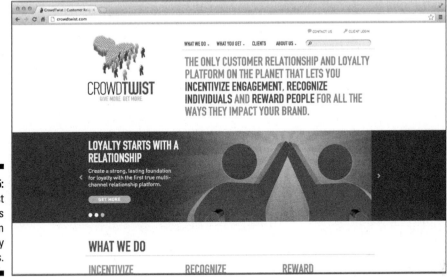

Figure 10-5:
CrowdTwist
focuses
more on
monetary
rewards.

Gigya

Gigya (www.gigya.com) offers a platform for making Web sites more social in a variety of ways, including game mechanics. You can use various Gigya modules independently or as a seamlessly integrated suite. Gigya, which also offers a social analytics dashboard, serves a wide range of customers, including ABC, Pepsi, and Verizon.

IActionable

IActionable (www.iactionable.com; see Figure 10-6) proudly touts its Engage Engine, viewed as one of the most flexible in the industry. Using this scalable system, you can create reward systems — complete with points, achievements, levels, leaderboards, and notifications — that are easy to learn but difficult to master. In addition, IActionable's fully customizable analytics tools enable you to track the metrics that matter to *you*.

Figure 10-6:
The
IActionable
Web site.

Seriosity

At Seriosity (www.seriosity.com), co-founders Byron Reeves and Leighton Read are Big Names in gamification — so much so that they wrote a book about it. (We talk more about the book *Total Engagement* in Chapter 14.) Their bag: Offering "consulting services to help enterprises develop a game strategy optimized for their challenges and workforce."Seriosity also offers a set of software products to help clients gamify their users' experiences.

Building: Finding Open-Source Resources

If you do opt to build your own gamification program, we can tell you about a few open-source resources that can help.

Not familiar with open source? Simply put, *open source* refers to a software development method in which everyday users are permitted to study, change, and improve the source code. This is in contrast to a typical commercial, proprietary software development model, in which the source code is closely guarded by the copyright holder.

✔ **Mozilla's Open Badges project:** Offered by Mozilla, the Open Badges project (`www.openbadges.org`; see Figure 10-7) makes it easy for anyone to issue, earn, and display badges through a shared infrastructure that's free and open to everyone. Badges are portable — that is, those who earn badges can display them on, say, their personal resume, Web site, social networking profile, or on employment sites.

✔ **CloudCaptive's UserInfuser platform:** From the makers of AppScale, UserInfuser — a scalable, open-source gamification platform — provides customizable gamification elements for badging, points, live notifications, and leaderboards. The platform, which is scalable, also includes analytics for tracking user participation. The result: increased user interaction.

✔ **Zurmo:** If you're looking to gamify a CRM system, then Zurmo (`www.zurmo.org`; see Figure 10-8), an open-source CRM application that is mobile, social, and gamified, may be for you. This flexible system claims to be easy to use and easy to customize, covering a wide variety of use cases out of the box.

Figure 10-7:
Open Badges provides open source badges.

Image courtesy of Mozilla

Figure 10-8:
Zurmo
covers a
variety of
CRM use
cases.

Chapter 11

Key Expertise for Your Gamification Team

Regardless of whether you opt to build your gamification system from the ground up or partner with a gamification provider to design and implement your program, you'll want to assemble a top-notch team to see it through. But who, exactly, are the peeps who should comprise that team?

To help you answer that question, this chapter outlines the key people you need to have on board to get your program off the ground and running.

Some team members might be internal — that is, employees in your organization. Others could be external — for example, consultants from a gamification provider or other third party.

Recognizing Key Stakeholders

A successful gamification team is composed of key stakeholders (note the plural here — it's never just one person) who

✔ Understand the business objectives.

✔ Have the authority to make decisions.

✔ Understand the systems with which the gamification system is being integrated.

✔ Have a vision for the gamification program.

Broadly speaking, these team members will include the following:

- Business champions
- Nerds
- Creative types

Bringing Together Business Champions

First and foremost, you need a business champion. A *business champion* is someone who has identified business objectives that he or she wants to achieve and possibly even the behaviors that will help achieve those objectives. The business champion also recognizes that gamification can help drive those behaviors.

Sometimes, your business champion will need a little convincing. In that case, don't bother trying to persuade him with impersonal software demos. Instead, try to find real company examples that highlight how gamification solved a pain point that that person knows all too well.

The identity of that business champion will vary from situation to situation. If, for example, the gamification efforts will center around motivating a sales force to action, then the business champion might be the VP of sales. If, on the other hand, the gamification program pertains to learning management, the business champion might be the head of HR. For a community site, the business champion will likely be the VP of community. Or it could be that the business champion is simply the director of business development.

Typically, identifying the right champions means finding people who have the specific pain point you're trying to address with your gamification system. For example, if it's the chief marketing officer, that person might have a challenge with ensuring customer loyalty. If the person is a vice-president of sales, maybe he or she cannot get the sales team to use its CRM software correctly.

Often, you won't have just a single business champion. You'll likely be working with several people on the business side who understand the business objectives and key behaviors involved. Chief among these will be a product person — someone who really understands the product in question and who wants to increase the use of certain product features. For a customer-facing property, other business champions might include the following:

- CMOs
- Heads of digital media
- Social media managers

In contrast, for an employee-facing property, the following people might be business champions:

- ✔ CIO
- ✔ VP of knowledge management
- ✔ VP of support and services

As you're assembling your key stakeholders, make it a point to get an executive champion on board. Gamification programs typically straddle multiple groups and systems, so you'll need someone with high-level authority on your side to make the necessary decisions and keep everyone in line.

Assembling Your Nerds

On the technical side of the gamification team, you need nerds with the knowledge to architect, develop, and test your gamification program. (You'll find out more about each of these phases in Chapter 12.) Ideally, they'll be skilled in the following technologies:

- ✔ **HTTP:** This web standard is the foundation for all data communication on the World Wide Web. HTTP is the method by which your gamification technologies will communicate with your web platform.

- ✔ **HTML:** HTML is a language for structuring and presenting content for the World Wide Web. The current version, HTML 5, supports all the latest multimedia, but remains easily readable by human types and computing devices alike. Figure 11-1 shows an example of HTML in action.

Figure 11-1:
The HTML code for the main page of a Web site.

Image courtesy of Badgeville

✔ **JavaScript:** This is a scripting language that can be used to build the various widgets that appear on a gamified site (we talk more about widgets in Chapter 12).

✔ **REST:** REST is less a technology and more a set of principles that define how various web standards, such as HTTP, are supposed to be used. The key characteristic of RESTful communication is that it's stateless. You make a request, you get a response, and you're done. Theoretically, if you adhere to REST principles, you'll end up with a system that plays nice with the web's architecture.

✔ **JSON data:** This is a text-based open standard for the exchange of data, usually between a server and a web application. JSON is derived from JavaScript — although it's language independent. It's designed to be readable by actual people.

You'll also need someone who understands how to integrate the gamification program with your back end — in other words, someone who understands the platform on which the Web property is built. There are hundreds of platforms you could gamify. Examples of platforms and the corresponding skills needed to work in them include the following:

✔ **WordPress:** WordPress environments typically require someone with the ability to read and manipulate JavaScript code.

✔ **SharePoint:** If you're gamifying a Microsoft Sharepoint property, you'll need someone who understands SharePoint and has .NET experience.

✔ **Oracle:** An Oracle system requires an understanding of Java.

✔ **Salesforce.com:** Salesforce.com apps run off the Force.com platform and Apex code.

If you're working with a gamification provider, that provider may offer a *connector* — that is, a pre-built piece of code that handles the various aspects of integration with your back end. If a connector is available to you, that means you don't need so much in the way of technical expertise on your team.

Gathering Creative Types

If you're a fan of the popular TV show *The Big Bang Theory*, you might remember the episode in which Dr. Sheldon Cooper finds himself in traffic court. Rather than simply pay his fine, he presents his defense: "Like a milking stool, my case rests on three legs." Similarly, a gamification team is comprised of three key categories of stakeholders. You're already familiar with two of them — business champions and nerds. In this section, you identify the third leg of your gamification milking stool: creative types. These can include the following:

- **Producer:** This person manages the process of designing and implementing your gamification program. She keeps people organized, facilitates communication, tracks the schedule, and so forth. There's a good chance that if you're reading this book, you're in the role of the producer.

- **Designer:** This is the person who decides what the user experience will be, decides which framework will be used, balances the system, etc. This may be the same person as the producer, but maybe not.

- **Graphic artist:** Your team will be severely lacking without a good graphic artist on board. Why? Because many gamification programs rely heavily on visual elements, such as badges. As you we mention in Chapter 5, badges should be eye-catching works of art. Ergo, you need an artist. Most importantly, your visual elements should map to the look and feel of the digital environment that you're gamifiying.

It's best to work with artists who are already schooled in web design. They know up front not to design super-elaborate graphics. (When intricate pieces get shrunk down to badge size, all that detail is inevitably lost.)

- **Brand manager:** This person understands and is responsible for maintaining the look and feel of a brand. You want him or her on your side as you develop your gamification program to make sure that what you come up with is in line with the brand being gamified.

- **Content developer:** Yes, you *could* launch a gamification program without a content developer. But having one on your team, even if that person also fulfills another role (such as designer or brand manager), will help you develop the program — especially the text used in notifications, badge names, level names, and other messaging. That person need not be a Writer with a capital W. Anyone with a knack for "structuring interesting word usements" (to paraphrase Steve Martin in the delightful 1991 film *L.A. Story*) will do.

Identifying Nice-to-Have Team Members

In addition to the *key* roles outlined so far, there may be some *nice-to-have* team members for any gamification program. These folks aren't strictly necessary, but having them around can do wonders as you perform the hard task of designing and developing your program:

- ✔ **Social game designer:** Not to be confused with a social media expert or even a producer, a social game designer is someone with the skills to design an actual game. Although most gamification efforts aren't of the social game variety, having someone with this background can make it easier to devise a clever and eye-catching program.

- ✔ **Behavior psychologist:** The purpose of your gamification program is to drive certain behaviors that will help you achieve specific business objectives. Having someone on hand with insight into these behaviors is sure to give you helpful insights as you work.

- ✔ **Loyalty expert:** For a customer-facing property, a loyalty expert — someone who is well-versed in programs developed to foster customer loyalty — can be helpful. This might simply be a marketing person with knowledge in that area. Gamification programs typically reward valuable behaviors, so they can intersect with traditional loyalty programs.

- ✔ **Enterprise engagement or business process expert:** A person with knowledge in this area can be quite useful for an employee-facing property. That's because if you're looking to gamify a business application, it's helpful to know the key business processes you should gamify with game mechanics like missions.

Chapter 12

Ready, Set, Go! Configuring and Deploying Gamification Elements

During the course of this book, you've learned all about the theory behind gamification — how game mechanics can help you motivate your customers or employees to perform behaviors that will advance your business objectives. Now it's time to roll up your sleeves and get cracking.

This chapter outlines the major steps in implementing any gamification program. Without getting too technical (you're welcome), it identifies the key activities involved in gamifying your business, in all the various stages. If you're ready to implement gamification in your organization, read on.

It probably goes without saying that gamification programs can be quite complex. But don't freak out. Identifying the major stages in the project can help you wrap your brain around what needs to be done, and in what order. These stages are as follows:

✔ Design

✔ Development

✔ Testing

✔ Implementation

After that, you'll generally repeat this cycle as needed, based on the results you achieve.

Design of the Times: The Design Stage

You'll need to put on your thinking cap — or at the very least some pondering earmuffs — during the design stage. In this phase, you must determine what your business objectives are and devise a gamification program that will help you meet those objectives.

Identifying business objectives

Chapter 3 discusses the importance of identifying your business objectives before embarking on a gamification program. Unless you're in some sort of scenario like the one in the movie *Major League* (you own the Cleveland Indians and you want the team to lose so you can move it somewhere warm, for example), you must identify what you want to achieve through your gamification program. In other words, what business problem do you want to solve?

Maybe you want to increase engagement. Or maybe you want to improve employee performance. Only after you've identified what you want to achieve can you design a gamification program to help you meet that goal.

For more about identifying business objectives, review Chapter 3.

Designing a gamification program

Designing a gamification program involves the following steps:

- ✔ Choosing a framework
- ✔ Selecting behaviors to reward
- ✔ Defining levels and points
- ✔ Defining rules for achievements
- ✔ Choosing rewards
- ✔ Designing the gamification elements

Choosing a framework

As detailed in the chapters in Part II, a *framework* is a collection of game mechanics that are known to work well together. There are many ways to organize game mechanics, and that organization will set the tone for how your users interact with your site.

You have a couple approaches when it comes to deciding which program is right for you. One is to consider whether your audience consists of customers or employees. If your site is for customers, ask yourself whether there is a community on your site. If so, is it cooperative or competitive in nature?

If the experience of your site is more solo than social in nature, you'll probably want to opt for the social loyalty framework. If it's social and cooperative in nature, you'll probably choose the community expert framework. If it's social and competitive, then the competitive pyramid framework is probably the best fit.

If your site is for employees, you want to consider whether they'll be best served by a prescriptive, hand-holding style; a cooperative, employee-to-employee mentoring approach; or a team-versus-team scenario (a friendly competition to increase motivation). If the site should be prescriptive (it holds the user's hand as it walks them through a series of steps), opt for the gentle guide framework. For a mentoring program, go with company collaborator. For the friendly competition scenario, choose company challenge.

Chapter 7 covers frameworks and how to decide which one is right for you.

Selecting behaviors to reward

Your users perform behaviors on your site or in your application. They log in, read pages, watch videos, create content, review content, and so on. Based on your business goals, you can decide which behaviors you want users to perform and reward them for performing those behaviors. With this high-fidelity data, you can generate basic reporting and rich analytics to find top users and identify opportunities for improvement.

Behaviors have basic properties, such as a name and a point value that users receives when they perform the behavior. You can also contextualize user behaviors with metadata. For example, if you're tracking when users write product reviews, you may want to record the product being reviewed. Tracking with metadata enriches your behavior data, enabling powerful and flexible options for crediting behavior and granting rewards.

The minute you decide what behaviors you want to reward, you should start tracking them. Not sure what to reward? Start tracking behaviors anyway, so you can see which ones your users gravitate toward already. For more on tracking behaviors, see Chapter 13.

Defining levels and points

As you saw in Chapter 6, levels represent status and indicate progress. Typically, players advance to a new level when they earn a certain number of points. For example, after a player earns his first 50 points, he might be bumped up from the first level to the second. Then players might be bumped to the third level after crossing the 150-point threshold.

Levels tied to point thresholds generally hold true for site-wide reputation systems. But you might want to have community expert tracks that show a person's reputation for specific content, processes, or products (see Chapter 9 for more info). Those can be tied to performing specific behaviors rather than just points.

So you could be a Level 2 Apprentice on a clothing site (site-wide, tied to overall points) as well as a Tier 5 Cobbler based on behaviors performed in the shoe section. (If one system is global, and another is expertise-specific, it's a good idea to mix up the verbiage that describes the levels in these systems to avoid confusion.)

Defining rules for achievements

Rules are a set of conditions that must be met to earn a reward. Rules have easy-to-understand components, such as *behavior* and *behavior count*. In addition, there are optional attributes to support defining richer, more complex rules.

When designing your gamification program, you can set many different kinds of rules. Here are a few examples:

- **Basic (one or more behaviors):** Basic rules might involve rewarding a behavior such as reading five pages or rewarding users who perform multiple behaviors a specified number of times. For example, you might have a single rule that rewards a user for reading a story, rating the story, and rating a comment five times.

- **Time-related:** A time-related rule will have . . . wait for it . . . a time component, such as reading five pages every day for one week.

- **Goal-based:** These rules involve a measureable winning condition — maybe saving $100 or losing 50 pounds.

- **Content-related:** This type of rule involves specific content — for example, reading a sponsored review.

- **Group-/team-related:** Rules like these reward users for performing certain behaviors as a group — maybe joining an exercise plan or winning a challenge *en masse*.

- **Results- or participation-related:** This type of rule rewards users for achieving certain types of results — for example, finishing a competition in the top 10 or the 10th percentile.

- **Check-in–related:** A check-in-related rule rewards users for performing a check-in at (or close to) a specified location.

Choosing rewards

As Chapter 5 says, a *reward* is a virtual or tangible prize a user earns for performing desired behaviors. Rewards are associated with a collection of behaviors that supports an objective. Successful gamification hinges on the use of rewards.

To recap, rewards come in three categories:

- ✔ **Recognition:** Who doesn't want to be recognized for their achievements? No one, that's who. That's why recognition is part of just about every type of competition on the planet. Generally speaking, recognition encourages engagement and increases repetition — both of which are probably in your list of business objectives. Recognition is conferred in two ways: reputation and status.

- ✔ **Privileges:** Some users are motivated by receiving privileges. These might include early/VIP access, moderation powers, and stronger votes.

- ✔ **Monetary rewards:** Examples of monetary rewards include discounts, free shipping, prizes, and redemptions.

Chapter 5 gets way into the nitty-gritty of determining what types of rewards will work best for your gamification program. Rather than rehashing all that here, we'll just refer you there — specifically to the section "Choosing Rewards."

The playmaker: Designing the gamification elements

You've identified your business objectives. You've determined what behaviors will help drive those objectives and their associated rules. Now it's time to design your gamification elements.

The elements don't need to be terribly complex. In fact, it's probably better if they aren't. But it needs to be clear to users that they're being recognized or acknowledged for performing behaviors. That means basic points are essential, as is rewarding users who perform specific behaviors. For example, if a user shares something on Facebook or tweets something, that person might complete the Social Butterfly Mission.

Developing Nation: The Development Stage

Broadly speaking, the development stage involves the following tasks:

- ✔ Creating a site
- ✔ Defining behaviors

✔ Creating rewards

✔ Adding widgets

✔ Creating missions and tracks

Of course, the way you complete each of these tasks varies widely depending on whether you've opted to build your own gamification program from the ground up or partner with a gamification provider (or some combination of the two).

If you've opted to go your own route, you'll employ any one of various technologies to build the various components of your program. For rendering front-end gamification elements, you'll need to have someone who can work with JavaScript. If you're integrating your gamification elements with specific business software, you'll need someone with experience in the development language or framework that program was built on.

Development languages and frameworks might include the following:

✔ .NET (SharePoint and Microsoft)

✔ Java (Salesforce.com, Oracle, and other enterprise software providers)

✔ Ruby on Rails (many modern Web applications)

The programming language or framework you use will depend largely on what type of system you're working with. If it's a SharePoint site, you'll go with .NET. If it's SalesForce, you'll likely go with Java or Apex.

If, on the other hand, you've chosen a gamification provider, you'll be able to use that provider's tools to set things up, usually accessible via a user-friendly graphical user interface (GUI).

Unfortunately, coverage of the ins and outs of all these various approaches isn't possible here; we'll simply discuss some of the concepts behind them and show you a few examples of user interface elements representing the features being implemented.

Creating a site

You can use your gamification program on any number of web sites or applications. For example, you can create a site and associate it with a given URL — say, mysite.com. Then, you can use the same gamification program for other sites, also. In other words, you can use a gamification program you create for mysite.com with myothersite.com and with mobile applications.

The first thing you should do is to create a sample site along with some behaviors, rewards, and missions, just to get your feet wet. After that, you should dry off your feet.

Defining behaviors

By now, we hope you have a very solid idea of what behaviors you want to define. Why? Because it's time to actually define them. Often, a behavior is defined as a name, a point value, and a time limit. In addition, behaviors may have the following properties:

- **Cooldown:** This is the time, typically in seconds, that must pass before the user can be rewarded for performing the same behavior again. This number is based on an estimate of how long it takes a user to perform the given behavior. This is simply one anti-gaming mechanic designed to prevent abuse of the gamification program.

- **Iconography:** This refers to the informative pop-ups that are associated with certain behaviors. A pop-up could appear as a notification, as a reward, or even to explain rules or which behaviors are worth points. It reinforces the desired behaviors, reminds the user that the game exists, gives feedback for another step in the right direction, communicates the points value of the behavior, and so on. Figure 12-1 shows an example of a pop-up.

- **Activity stream text:** In gamification systems with a social component, notifications of rewards given are displayed in an accompanying activity stream. By default, these notifications say something along the lines of, "<player name><did something> on <page title>," where the bracketed text serves as placeholders for the actual text. You can, of course, change this notification to be whatever you like.

Figure 12-1:
Pop-ups give users feedback about valuable behaviors.

Image courtesy of Badgeville

You must do more than simply define a behavior, however. You must take a few additional steps to manage behaviors.

- **Defining filters:** A *filter* determines whether an incoming behavior matches a defined behavior. For example, suppose you want to reward users for adding money to a savings plan. A filter will help to determine whether a user has performed that behavior — for example, ignoring when money is added to a checking account or brokerage account.

- **Defining units:** The units component of a behavior has two properties: name and value. Perhaps the most obvious example of a unit would be the ubiquitous *mile*, given in airline rewards programs. You can create any type of defining unit you want. The value is the amount of that unit to reward when the behavior is performed.

- **Defining behavior eligibility:** If you've implemented anti-gaming mechanisms — rate limiting, count limiting, and so forth — then you'll need to define this property to determine whether a behavior is eligible for reward.

Creating rewards and levels

Creating rewards is conceptually simple: You specify the behavior you want to reward, define any rules associated with the behavior (or behaviors), and then indicate what reward corresponds to that behavior. You'll also want to associate an image with the reward.

As mentioned previously, there are various types of rewards: recognition, status, and monetary. These might be further categorized as *tangible* (monetary) and *virtual* (recognition and status). This section focuses on the creation of virtual rewards — think badges and levels.

If the behavior you want to reward is an advanced behavior rather than a simple one, you can configure various properties as needed.

To refresh your memory, a *simple behavior* is one that doesn't require additional qualifiers to describe. Examples of simple behaviors might include commenting or responding to a customer inquiry. An *advanced behavior* is a simple behavior with one or more qualifiers. Advanced behaviors might include commenting on an article about fashion or responding to a customer inquiry within 30 minutes of receiving it.

For example, you might set the following properties:

- Whether the reward should be given to an individual user or to a group, or team, of users

- Whether the reward can be earned more than once

✔ How many times a reward can be earned

✔ When the reward can be earned

Figure 12-2 shows the creation of an advanced behavior using a gamification provider's interface.

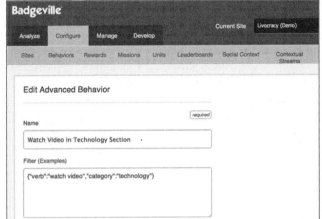

Figure 12-2:
Creating an
advanced
behavior.

Image courtesy of Badgeville

Some gamification platforms let you copy rules you've already created — a real timesaver.

To create a level, you define a name, a starting point value, an image, a hint, and a message — for example, "Congratulations! You're really making a name for yourself. Don't stop now, you've got room to grow!"

Technically, you can redefine levels as necessary. That said, we recommend that you avoid changing level definitions in such a way that you demote users. It's more common to add new levels as necessary.

Adding widgets

Many gamification providers provide a suite of widgets that you can embed in your site to educate, encourage, and guide users. The point of using widgets is that they're crazy easy to implement. (Of course, there's a downside, too: They can be a bit generic and are less likely to fit perfectly with your existing site.)

Examples of widgets you might add to your gamification program include the following:

✔ **Activity feed widget:** An activity feed widget displays achievements unlocked by users in a continually updated stream. This widget serves a few purposes: creating a dynamic, live feeling to the site, advertising available rewards, and giving users recognition (see Figure 12-3).

✔ **Missions widget:** This type of widget displays all missions in which a user is currently engaged (see Figure 12-4). Mission progress should be clearly indicated numerically and with a visual progress bar. In addition, this widget should list all missions available for a user. Ideally, clicking a mission opens the mission widget, which displays all rewards in the mission (more on missions later in this chapter).

✔ **Showcase widget:** The showcase widget is a collection of progress and stats. A list of missions is a component of the showcase. Each mission card opens a mission widget, where you can see all of the achievements/rewards in the mission. You would use this type of widget on a profile page, because it represents a member's rewards-based identity and status. It also provides access to collections and missions, which helps to guide users along (see Figure 12-5).

Figure 12-3:
A widget was used to create this activity feed.

Image courtesy of Badgeville

Figure 12-4:
A missions widget can be employed to help users keep abreast of the various missions in which they are involved.

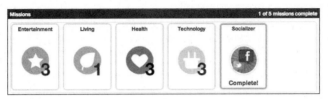

Image courtesy of Badgeville

Figure 12-5:
Showcase widgets work best on a user's profile page.

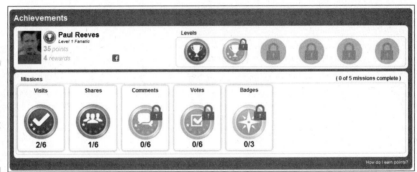

Image courtesy of Badgeville

✔ **Rewards widget:** A rewards widget contains a user profile summary, recent achievements, access to a showcase widget, and access to a settings widget.

✔ **Settings widget:** A settings widget allows your user to configure options like selecting a profile image and enabling/disabling browser and e-mail notifications.

✔ **Header widget:** A header widget displays the user name, profile picture, points, and level information. As users navigate and use your site, their points increase in real time. This widget, which is designed to be added inline to an existing header on your page, brings great visibility to your rewards program. It educates users about your rewards program and, as points continually increase, it encourages continued on-site activity (see Figure 12-6). The header tab widget is similar (see Figure 12-7). The header tab widget offers all the same benefits as the header widget, but in a self-contained block, placed on a static location on your site.

Figure 12-6:
A header widget encourages activity on your site.

Image courtesy of Badgeville

Figure 12-7:
Header tab widgets are similar to header widgets.

Image courtesy of Badgeville

✔ **Player card widget:** Like the header widget, this type of widget is designed to communicate member identity succinctly and prominently. The player card contains a user profile image on the left along with her numeric level; on the right is other information such as display name, level, and points (see Figure 12-8).

Figure 12-8:
Player card widgets serve the same basic purpose as header widgets and header tab widgets.

Image courtesy of Badgeville

✔ **Leaderboard widget:** With this type of widget, the top users for the configured time slice are displayed (see Figure 12-9). This widget can be used when you want to prominently advertise the rewards program and advertise its social nature. It creates a social layer and provides instant community around achievement and rewards. Similar to a leaderboard widget is a multi-leaderboard widget, which displays the top users for all available time slices — for example, daily, weekly, monthly, and all time, as shown in Figure 12-10. This provides more contextual views — and thus more chances for a given user to appear as a top community member.

Figure 12-9: An example of a leaderboard.

Image courtesy of Badgeville

Figure 12-10: A multi-leaderboard widget offers more contextual views.

Image courtesy of Badgeville

✔ **Multitab widget:** A multitab widget is essentially a hybrid, melding a leaderboard widget with a rewards widget. Again, the rewards widget in turn offers access to a showcase widget and a settings widget (see Figure 12-11).

Figure 12-11:
Multitab
serves a
dual
purpose.

✔ **Levels widget:** This type of widget displays all unlocked and locked
levels in a single display (see Figure 12-12). It's excellent for gamification
programs in which level progression is critical.

Figure 12-12:
If your
gamification
program
emphasizes
level pro-
gression,
add a levels
widget to the
interface.

Some gamification providers let you alter their widgets by customizing the
look and feel. Some even help you to design your own. If your styling requirements can only be met through CSS, you may be able to create a CSS file and
override existing styles as necessary. You then link to the CSS file as you normally would.

Notice how a lot of the widgets listed are the same as the game mechanics discussed in Chapter 6. Simply looking at the list of available widgets can help you with your game design!

Adding missions and tracks

You can use missions to guide players through an experience or to encourage ongoing participation.

Configuring a mission is a simple matter of stringing together a series of existing rewards in whatever order you prefer. You can also name the mission and indicate the mission type — progression or random. If you like, you might include an image for the mission, as well as text to describe the purpose of the mission and the number of points you will earn if you complete it (if applicable).

Optionally, you can configure these additional properties:

✔ Whether the mission can be completed more than once

✔ How many times the mission can be completed

✔ When the mission should be made available

Just as a mission is a series of rewards strung together, a *track* — often used in the community expert and gentle guide frameworks — is a series of missions strung together.

You create a track by adding active missions to it. As with creating missions, you must also name the track and specify whether it's a progression (ordered) or is random (unordered) in nature. Again, as with missions, you can include an image for the track as well as text to describe the purpose of the track. Optionally, you can specify a time interval in which the track must be completed.

Testing 1, 2, 3: The Testing Stage

You don't stage a Broadway show before the general public until you've run through a dress rehearsal or two. Likewise, you shouldn't go live with your gamification program until you've tested it to make sure it works the way you want it to.

In general, the testing phase is pretty straightforward. You simply put the program through its paces in a sandbox setting — that is, an internal testing environment. This phase might also involve A/B testing (or comparing different versions of the gamification program to determine which one is most effective).

Testing is an iterative program, and should continue after you go live. That is, you launch, see what works, listen for feedback, watch what your users do, and use analytics to monitor, tune, and optimize. (The subject of analytics is covered in Chapter 13.) Be open to making adjustments!

Live It Up: Going Live

After your program has been tested, it's time to go live. This is when you'll turn to the member of your team who has some understanding of the ins and outs of your web platform and the tools needed to connect it to your gamification platform.

Most of the connections between your web platform and gamification platform involve understanding the API of each system. With most modern web systems, you're typically dealing with RESTAPIs. (REST refers to a stateless way of communicating between systems using HTTP in some standardized format.)

Some gamification providers do this difficult work for you, providing a connector. *Connectors* are pre-built pieces of code that handle the various aspects of integration, making the gamification program a turnkey affair. Indeed, as gamification technology continues to advance, these types of turnkey solutions will become more prevalent.

From start to finish, most gamification programs take anywhere from 30 days to three months to implement.

Stay Safe Out There: A Word on Security

Not to get all Chicken Little on you, but you really *must* take measures to secure the data you gather with your gamification program.

Network-related security features

Creating distinct user roles for each account and implementing a variety of network security options will help you to ensure that your data is secure when managing your gamification program.

On the topic of user roles in your admin system, we recommend implementing the following roles:

- **Admin:** Those with admin privileges have the power to administer the network, which includes creating, editing, or deleting other accounts as well as modifying security settings. When employees leave the company, you can easily revoke their access to your gamification program.

- **User:** If an employee will be working on your gamification platform but does not need the ability to administer the network, the user role is appropriate.

- **Read only:** You might assign the read-only role to someone who just needs to view reports, or to outside vendors or contractors.

With regard to network security options, we suggest you take the following steps to limit hooliganism on your system:

- **Limit failed login attempts:** Determine how many login attempts are allowed and, when this number is exceeded, lock out the offending account until an admin unlocks it.

- **Log out the account after a certain amount of time:** If, after x minutes, no activity occurs on the account, shut that puppy down.

- **Enable IP whitelisting:** Whitelisting means to authorize access. Enabling IP whitelisting restricts access to your network to only those IP addresses (or to a range of addresses) you choose.

- **Require strong passwords:** If you're one of those people who just uses their dog's name as a password, a pox be upon you. These days, passwords should be a minimum of eight characters and contain at least one alpha and one numeric character. For even stronger passwords, go for a minimum of 12 characters, with at least one alpha, one numeric, and one special character.

  Special characters include the ones used in comic strips to denote foul language — think !@#$%^&*()-_+=~`|\{}[]:";'<>?,./ and \.)

  On the subject of passwords, you should require users to change their passwords on a semi-regular basis, and you should not permit users to reuse old passwords after they've been changed.

Generally speaking, authentication isn't something that happens on the gamification side. Rather, authentication occurs on the web platform side. That is, users log in to your site using that site's authentication procedure; once they do, the gamification elements are automatically made available to them.

Platform-related security features

We don't want to freak you out by getting too technical, but you should be aware that in addition to implementing network-related security features, there are a few platform features that prevent system misuse. These can include the following:

- ✔ **Private and public API keys:** For calls that involve crediting users or creating and managing rewards, you can use a private key for server-to-server communication that isn't visible to end-users. Using this private key in conjunction with SSL (mentioned momentarily) provides significant security without affecting performance. You can use the public key with the JS API to quickly enable a powerful visualization layer.

- ✔ **Read and write APIs:** Using read and write APIs is a fancy way of saying you can get, post, push, and delete data. Thus, you have endpoints that let you list or read data. You have other endpoints that let you create, update, and delete. Usually, read-only APIs refer to read-only API keys.

- ✔ **SSL:** Short for Secure Sockets Layer, SSL is a cryptographic protocol that provides security for communication over the Internet by encrypting segments of network connections.

For best results, you can use a combination of these features to ensure your experience is secure.

Chapter 13

Analyze This: Understanding Analytics

Questions: How do you know that the gamification program you put in place is actually driving the behaviors you need to occur in order to meet your business objectives? How do you know that it's providing you with the desired return on investment (ROI)?

One critical part to these answers is analytics. Broadly speaking, *analytics* is the use of technology, research, and statistics to identify and solve problems — specifically, problems in business and industry. Analytics is the essential link between operations and business decisions. Using analytics, you can assess the success (or lack thereof) of any business operation.

Analytics is the process of setting up these essential business measurements, monitoring them on an ongoing basis, and feeding the results back to the most appropriate consumer in the most appropriate manner.

Good analytics is not about recording and measuring everything and producing numerous and complicated reports and dashboards. It's about narrowing in on what really drives the business objectives and surfacing it in the best, most easily digestible way possible.

Of course, what's important varies by business unit and each individual case. One organization may be interested in getting more users to visit the site and load multiple pages. Another might be all about getting core users to return regularly, to tweet about what they saw, or to buy something from a sponsor.

(See Chapter 3 for more on pinpointing your business objectives and Chapter 4 for help determining what behaviors align with which business objectives.)

In this chapter, you discover just what activities are involved in analytics, the key metrics to measure, and what kinds of information you can glean from a solid analytics platform.

Understanding Analytics-Related Activities

Think of a typical product cycle. You design something, build it, measure the results, and tweak it — and then start the process all over again (see Figure 13-1).

Analytics is what lets you close that loop. Using analytics, you can measure whether your gamification program is having the desired effect. Analytics can also help you pinpoint where the problems with your program lie. Is the design off? Did you reward the wrong behaviors? And once you've identified where the problems lie, analytics can help you determine how to correct them. In today's high-tech world, it's all about optimization, and that's exactly what analytics allows you to do.

Figure 13-1:
A typical product cycle.

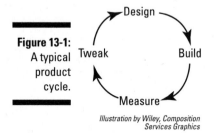

Illustration by Wiley, Composition Services Graphics

Successful analytics involves the following activities:

- ✔ Measuring
- ✔ Tracking
- ✔ Aggregating
- ✔ Analyzing
- ✔ Reporting

These activities might occur with every aspect of an organization's performance, from product deployment to customer satisfaction.

Choosing the right analytics tool

One tool people use for analytics purposes is Google Analytics. Google Analytics is great at telling you where people come from and where they go after visiting your site. It's less adept, however, at telling you what they're doing while they're there. Enter gamification. When you use a solid gamification provider, you don't just provide users with meaningful feedback such as acknowledgments and rewards on their behavior; you also record every activity at a user level. And what can be recorded or tracked can be analyzed.

Using integrated tools supplied by your gamification provider, you can identify a specific user's activities. You can tell whether the same users who played a week ago also played today, or whether the same users who like to share on Facebook also tend to be the ones who come back to the site most frequently. You can segment users based on what they do. With gamification, you can begin to understand all sorts of relationships among the different pieces of data you capture.

Tracking behaviors

Remember earlier in the book, when we said that you should start tracking behaviors, like, pronto, even before you put your program in place? As you plan your gamification program, it's smart to implement a *bake-in period* — a phase during which you track existing behaviors before you start handing out rewards and displaying notifications. That's so that once your gamification program takes shape, you can use analytics to determine how effective it is by comparing your *before* results — your benchmarks — with your *after* results. Ideally, you're looking for what we call *lift*, or an improvement in your results (see Figure 13-2). The higher the average visit frequency on your site, the shorter the bake-in period can be (see Table 13-1).

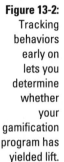

Figure 13-2: Tracking behaviors early on lets you determine whether your gamification program has yielded lift.

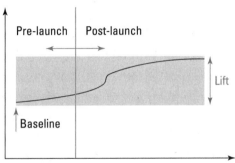

Illustration by Wiley, Composition Services Graphics

Table 13-1	Suggested Lengths of Bake-in Periods
Average Visit Frequency	*Length of Bake-in Period*
Weekly	Two weeks
Every two to three weeks	Three weeks
Monthly	Four weeks

Store as much raw data (and metadata around a particular behavior) as you can at the lowest level possible (per player, per activity) to keep your options open for future insights. From a technical perspective, tracking behaviors is relatively simple. You get a user ID, you note the time, and you capture what behavior the person performed or what reward the user received. That said, you must plan carefully to ensure you're capturing the *right* data. In other words, you must target the appropriate behaviors to get the data you want. For more information about behaviors, see Chapter 4.

Behavior tracking, which is invisible to the user, enables you to assess and fine-tune your gamification program both before users become actively involved in the game experience as well as after.

Measuring behaviors

At its core, analytics is about measurements. Without measurements, it's impossible to tell what you're doing well and, more importantly, in what areas you could stand to improve. Failing to take measurements makes it impossible to adjust to change.

You can use analytics to measure any number of business drivers. For your gamification program, though, analytics will focus on behavior. Behavior analytics provides you with the data, context, and insight to understand how people engage with your Web site, mobile applications, and enterprise applications. Serving up rich behavior data, behavior analytics offers a window into what users actually *do*.

Don't get us wrong: Things like self-reported demographic data are great. But they're not as great as data about *actual activities* performed on a site or in a mobile app.

A gamification program with a robust behavior analytics component lets you both measure what users do on your site and drive change by providing behavioral incentives — making it both the agent of change and the measurement gauge. As you surface and drive users' behaviors, you magnify the separation between the various segments of your user population, effectively increasing your signal-to-noise ratio. With gamification, you provide the context and measure the effect, continuously adjusting as you go.

Aggregating data

During the aggregation process, you gather and organize your measurement data, expressing it in summary form for the purposes of analysis. In other words, you take all the raw data you've collected and arrange it in a meaningful way. For example, you might group measurements to glean data about a particular group of users, or to determine the frequency of a given behavior in a specific time span.

Data analysis

Essentially, what you're doing in this process is piecing together your data to form a story. Did your site traffic suddenly spike? Looking at various metrics and putting them in a larger context might help you explain this. Maybe it was because of a promotion your marketing department launched. Maybe it was because something on your site went viral on Facebook. The point is, with your data in hand, you can tell the story of exactly what happened and why.

Some people divide data analysis into the following categories:

- ✔ Exploratory data analysis (EDA)
- ✔ Confirmatory data analysis (CDA)

Exploratory data analysis (EDA)

Exploratory, by definition, implies looking for something you're not expecting to find. With EDA, you see patterns in the data — which is summarized in a visual manner, usually in graph form — that point to something potentially interesting. You then pursue those patterns and the relationships among them until you build a "story" that explains something you previously did not understand or highlights something you weren't aware of before.

An example might be as simple as a business user noticing a spike in daily users on her dashboard that seems out of the ordinary. There were no known causes for this — no marketing or PR campaigns — and it doesn't fit into the expected seasonal pattern. She asks analysts for help, and they produce multiple cuts on the data available to see if there are any potential leads. There might be a geographical aspect to the spike, or it may be localized to a single time of the day and originate from the same source on the Internet. Pursuing this chain of measurements may eventually expose a single tweet or a Facebook post that happened to be picked up at just the right time and spread virally across the web.

Another example might involve trying to establish a link between revenues and user activity on a site or in an application. It may not be driven by any particular change in the metrics, but simply by the desire to see if there are any strong indicators that may preemptively point to a greater tendency to pay for services. Because there's no initial hypothesis, and all the data is looked at as a whole, the analysis is an exploratory exercise — it may or may not lead to anything interesting. If it does, it could then generate a whole new set of questions. Exploratory analysis could also tell if the data in your possession actually contains valuable information, which could, for example, be used in building predictive models.

Confirmatory data analysis (CDA)

As its name suggests, *confirmatory* data analysis involves confirming a hypothesis (or not). You see something in the data, and you have an idea as to what is causing it. Or you know you did something that was aimed at a well-defined outcome, and you want to see the evidence that it worked. Maybe you ran a marketing campaign and want to confirm that it was successful in driving a new audience to your site. Or you introduced a new level to your gamification program and want to make sure it did, in fact, reinvigorate your advanced users, who were running out of things to do. Or you see a metric following what appears to be a time trend and want to test whether your understanding of its origin is correct.

It's quite rare, especially in the business world, to come across a true exploratory analysis; confirmatory data analysis is almost always used. Why? Businesses are results driven, and people generally tend to have an abundance of hypotheses about what works and what doesn't. In fact, it's hard for people to *not* form hypotheses. Even today, scientists generally build experiments to explore particular educated guesses or theories formed ahead of time. A true exploration these days often results from being completely stumped. When you really can't find any good hypotheses to chase, all you have left is to explore in the hopes of finding something that will set you on the right path.

Stay flexible. Learn and adjust as you go. There's no one-size-fits-all analytics solution.

Reporting your findings

It's not enough to simply analyze your data. Your findings must be reported to the decision makers in your organization so they can act on your information. Often, special software is used to generate these reports, which typically take the form of graphs, text, and/or tables, often presented in dashboard form, like the dials in the dashboard of your car (see Figure 13-3). These reports should give higher-ups quick insight into how well your gamification program is working.

Reporting is a very important aspect of business intelligence and knowledge management.

Figure 13-3:
Reporting,
dashboard-
style.

Image courtesy of Badgeville

Identifying Key Metrics

Let's start with the basics and lay out a simple framework for the different
types of metrics you should be paying attention to. What's a metric? Very
simply, it's a standard of measurement. These include the following:

- **User:** This is the 10,000,000-foot overview of your product. How many
  users do you have? Are you growing? Are you getting new users or
  re-engaging old ones? What's the demographic breakdown? Are you
  affected by daily/weekly/seasonal trends?

- **Retention:** Do you keep the users you bring in? For how long? Are certain areas retaining better than others? Are there times when you are
  significantly more or less successful?

- **Engagement:** What are your users doing? How often? Is their experience
  rich or stale? Are they progressing? Are certain activities performed
  much more (or less) than others? Are your users spreading the word?

Some people might add conversion to this list, but we'd argue that's a subset of user engagement, being just one more activity in a chain of engagement-related events. (*Conversion* can mean different things — from getting more registered users, to going viral, to getting click-throughs, to product purchases.) That being said, conversion remains a key metric.

The specific metrics discussed in the upcoming sections on user metrics, retention metrics, and engagement metrics are based on ones developed by Badgeville. They're used as examples to demonstrate how typical metrics work.

Working with user metrics

Ideally, your analytics system helps you analyze user-level metrics (see Figure 13-4) — for example, the basic size of the current user base.

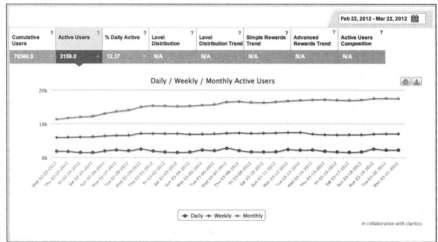

Figure 13-4: User metrics.

Image courtesy of Badgeville

In addition, you want your analytics system to show things like this:

- Current-points-earned distribution
- Visualization of level distribution over time
- Distribution of total rewards earned per user
- Cumulative-rewards-earned trend, by specific reward

Your analysis should also look at the active user composition over time in terms of how many users fall in and out of the active pool. Depending on the time interval, some users may be lapsing or inactive, whereas others are reactivating after being dormant for a while. The change in active user base from day to day is described by the number of new users acquired plus the number of users reactivated, less the number of lapsed users.

The fundamental questions being answered with user metrics are as follows:

- How healthy is your user base?
- Is it growing or shrinking, and why?
- Are users having trouble progressing through the levels of your gamification program?
- Can you identify bottlenecks or deviations from program design?

Examples of specific user-related metrics might include the following (remember, these are based on Badgeville's metrics):

- **Cumulative uniques:** Measures the total number of unique users seen in your data to date.
- **Daily/weekly/monthly active users:** Measures unique users seen on the given date or date range (see Figure 13-5).
- **Top *N*players.** This can be by the number of times an individual activity is performed in a given date range, by the total number of activities in a given date range (also listing individual activity counts), or by the number of points earned in a given date range (optionally listing all the rewards earned).
- **Players earning a reward:** Presented in a given date range.
- **Players completing a mission:** Presented in a given date range.
- **Players performing an activity:** Presented in a given date range. Can be broken down by a particular metadata key (by category, date, time, or some other piece of metadata — for more information about metadata, refer to Chapter 4, in the section "Comparing Simple and Advanced Behaviors.").
- **Weekly/Monthly active users composition:** This metric, which can be *trended* (displayed in such a way as to reveal a general tendency), tracks unique users seen in the week/month leading up to a given date. This information is broken down by user composition — that is, new, lapsed, dead, and reactivated.
- **Points:** Shows the current points distribution — that is, the number of users currently in possession of a given number of points. Outliers are rolled into the highest bin.

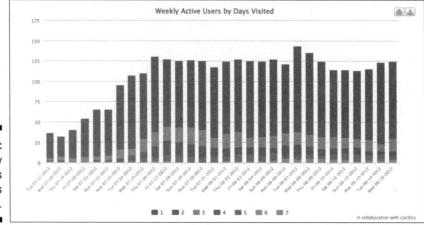

Figure 13-5:
Weekly
active users
by days
visited.

Image courtesy of Badgeville

✔ **Points by hour:** This metric, which can be trended, reveals the total and cumulative points earned by hour of a given day.

✔ **Levels:** Shows the current levels distribution — that is, the number of users currently at each defined level.

✔ **Levels over time:** This metric, which can be trended, indicates the composition of daily cumulative uniques in terms of users by level.

✔ **Levels over time normalized:** This metric, which can be trended, is a fraction representing the total cumulative uniques to date by level.

✔ **Achievements:** Shows the current achievements distribution — that is, the cumulative number of rewards by type received to date (see Figure 13-6).

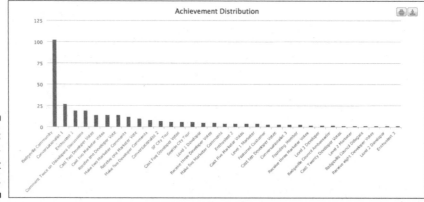

Figure 13-6:
Achieve-
ment
distribution.

Image courtesy of Badgeville

✓ **Rewards over time:** Shows the cumulative daily trend for each bar in the Achievements graph (see Figure 13-7).

✓ **Rewards earned distribution:** Shows the current number of players who have earned a given number of different rewards.

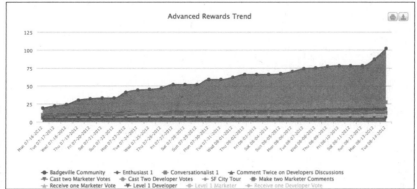

Figure 13-7:
Advanced
rewards
trend.

Image courtesy of Badgeville

Exploring engagement metrics

Engagement is the primary objective of most gamification programs. Engagement metrics are designed to measure the amount of interaction with the product in a given span of time.

When it comes to engagement metrics, you want to look at the following:

✓ Distribution of visit frequency

✓ Activities performed and users performing them (including per-user metrics, such as mean and median)

✓ The distribution of repeated activity counts

Figure 13-8 shows an example of engagement metrics.

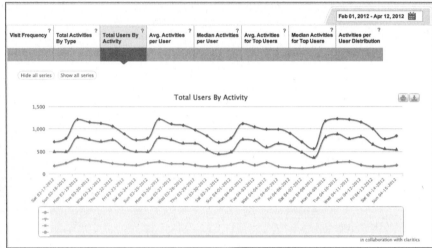

Figure 13-8:
Engagement
metrics.

Image courtesy of Badgeville

The fundamental questions being answered with engagement metrics are as follows:

✔ How often do users interact with the product?

✔ How involved is their interaction when they do interact?

✔ How likely are users to repeat the same activity?

✔ Are you moving the needle on the overall population or at least the top segment?

The idea is that gamification makes your site more fun, meaning users become more engaged — reading articles, adding comments, communicating with others on your site. That, in turn, makes them more inclined to visit your site more often and to spend more time on your site when they're there. And of course, the more time they spend on your site, the more likely they are to see ads and spend money there.

Examples of specific engagement-related metrics might include the following (remember, these are based on Badgeville's metrics):

✔ **Total activities:** Tracks the total number of activities performed on a given date.

✔ **Total rewards:** Tracks the total number of rewards earned on a given date.

✔ **Mean and median activities:** Tracks the mean and median activities per player on a given date, either overall or broken down by individual activity.

✔ **Mean and median rewards:** Tracks the mean and median rewards per player on a given date. It is restricted to players actually earning rewards.

✔ **Rewards by date:** This metric, which can be trended, tracks the total rewards earned and the number of users earning those rewards by date and type of reward.

✔ **Rewards by date point range:** Visual representation of the top 10 percent of users.

✔ **Actions distribution:** Tracks the current number of players who have performed an activity N times, by behavior.

✔ **Actions:** This metric, which can be trended, tracks the total activities performed and the number of users performing them by date and activity (see Figure 13-9).

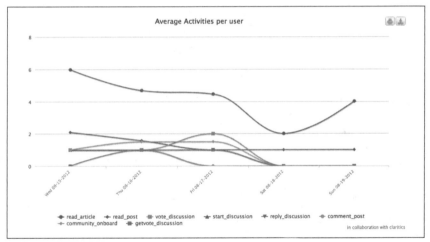

Figure 13-9:
Average
activities
per user.

Image courtesy of Badgeville

✔ **Actions by hour:** This metric, which can be trended, tracks the total activities performed by hour and by activity on a given day.

✔ **Rewards by hour:** This metric, which can be trended, tracks the total rewards earned by hour and by reward type on a given day.

Viewing retention metrics

Retention metrics enable you to gauge whether you're keeping or losing your users. Put another way, retention metrics measure the ability of your gamification program to increase the lifetime value of a user (see Figure 13-10). Simply put, a user's, or customer's, *lifetime value* is what that person is worth in monetary terms during the entire course of his or her relationship with a company. As users become more engaged with your platform, their lifetime value goes up.

Figure 13-10: Retention metrics.

Image courtesy of Badgeville

The fundamental questions being answered with retention metrics include the following:

✔ How many people come back to interact with the product after a certain interval?

✔ How many new users return to interact with the product after a certain interval?

Examples of specific retention-related metrics might include the following:

✔ **Daily/Weekly return rate:** This metric, which can be trended, shows the percentage of users who visited the site during the previous day or week who returned to the site on a given date or date range (see Figure 13-11).

Figure 13-11:
Daily return
rate.

✔ **Week Nretention:** This metric, which can be trended, shows the percentage of users seen for the first time in a given span who were seen again in the week leading up to (and including) a given date (see Figure 13-12).

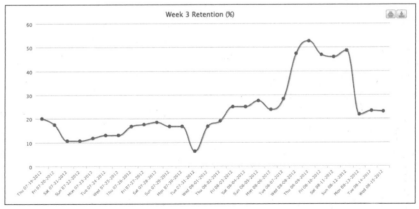

Figure 13-12:
Week
retention.

✔ **Play Frequency:** This metric, which can be trended, is a fraction dividing the number of weekly or monthly active users (for the week or month ending on a given date) by the number of days they visited the site.

Viewing metrics on a dashboard

A great way to see an overview of various key metrics is to view them on a dashboard. For example, the dashboard shown in Figure 13-13 presents the user with a quick overview of the user base in terms of total unique users ever seen as well as currently active users. Also shown are the daily return rate and week 1 retention, average play frequency per week, total activities performed, rewards earned by date, and the current snapshot of the level and achievement distributions.

Figure 13-13:
Viewing key metrics on a dashboard.

Image courtesy of Badgeville

Keep the user interface for viewing and understanding your analytics as simple as possible. Only display the metrics that matter, and keep them logically organized.

52 Pickup: Picking Your Metrics

Still not sure which metrics will apply best for your gamification program to achieve lift? Table 13-2 shows an industry-by-industry breakdown of key metrics that pertain to users, engagement, retention, and conversion.

Table 13-2		Managing and Measuring Lift		
Industry	*User*	*Engagement*	*Retention*	*Conversion*
Telco	Growth in user base	Frequency	Lifetime value	Registration
	Growth in active users	Number of activities	Churn reduction	ARPU
	Total unique users			
Tech	Growth in user base	Frequency	Lifetime value	Registrations
	Growth in active users	Number of activities	Retention	Course
	Total unique users			
Retail/ e-commerce	Growth in user base	Repeat visits	Lifetime value	Add to cart
	Growth in active users	Time to visit after purchase	Churn reduction	Purchase velocity
	Total unique users		Referral	Purchase amounts
CPG/consumer electronics	Growth in user base	Repeat visits	Lifetime value	Add to cart
	Growth in active users	Time to visit after purchase	Churn reduction	Purchase velocity
	Total unique users			Purchase amounts
Media	Growth in user base	Frequency	Active user growth	Page views
	Growth in active users	Number of activities	WAU grown	Video plays
	Total unique users	Virality (sharing)	Targeted referral	Sponsorship conversion
Health/ education	Growth in user base	Repeat visits	Increase life-time usage	Registration
	Growth in active users	Logging workouts	Lapsed user analysis	Increase in frequency
	Total unique users	Setting goals		

Q&A: Answering Critical Questions with Analytics

Here are some critical questions that can be answered with analytics:

✔ **How many users do you have?** This is a simple matter of finding cumulative users (anyone who has ever interacted with your site) and active users (users who are actively participating based on at least one activity in the last day/week/month). See Figure 13-14 for an example of a chart showing daily/weekly/monthly active users.

Figure 13-14: Finding out how many users you have.

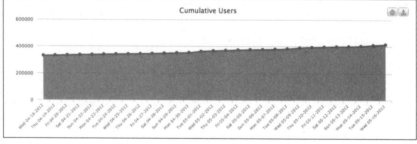

Image courtesy of Badgeville

✔ **How many new users do you get daily?** To determine this, view the change in cumulative users from day to day.

✔ **Are your users experiencing a healthy progression or getting stuck?** To gauge this, look for a current snapshot of the levels distribution or see how it has changed over time (see Figure 13-15). In the case of the former, you're looking for a chart that resembles a smooth exponential decay in the former. For the latter, you'd see a sizable (10+) percentage of higher levels (or increasing trend over time). Things to watch out for include big drops from one level to another, too few or too many levels, and users piling up at the highest level (meaning they've run out of things to do).

✔ **Do you have too few or too many rewards implemented or awarded?** An achievements distribution chart will help you answer this question. You'll want to watch for the same problems as with the levels distribution chart (refer to Figure 13-15). You can also look at the rewards-per-user trend in the user metrics (see Figure 13-16); as with levels, there should be a healthy mix of high and low achievers.

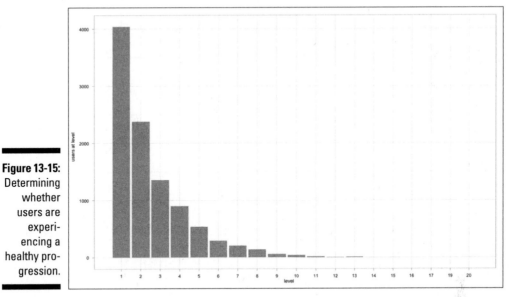

Figure 13-15: Determining whether users are experiencing a healthy progression.

Figure 13-16: You want a mix of high and low achievers.

✔ **How engaged are your users? Do you have power users?** A weekly visit frequency chart can help clear this up. Each date is represented by a stacked bar, where the height corresponds to weekly active users, and the color of each component corresponds to users who came in once, twice, or up to all seven days of the preceding week. The more users comprising the higher slices, the more active the user base is overall. You can also compare median activities per user, median activities for top users, and/or average activities for top users charts. If the median for top users is much higher than the median for everyone, you have a highly engaged core group of users. If the average for top users is much higher than the median, you have a few very engaged outliers even in that top segment (see Figure 13-17).

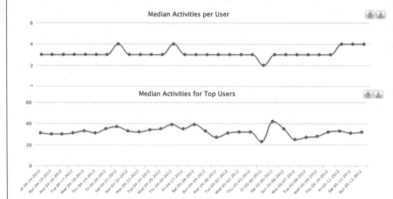

Figure 13-17:
Gauging
engage-
ment.

Image courtesy of Badgeville

Although it's good to have some power users, wide gaps between top achievers and the general population are generally not a healthy sign.

✔ **How much churn is there among your users?** You can answer this with an active users composition chart that shows weekly active users and breaks down the day-to-day change in terms of new users gained, users lapsing, and users reactivated after a period of lapse (see Figure 13-18). You can also look at the daily and weekly return rate to get a sense for how often people come back. A big difference between a daily rate and a weekly rate may be an indication of high churn, meaning people are likely interested in the short term but don't stick around very long.

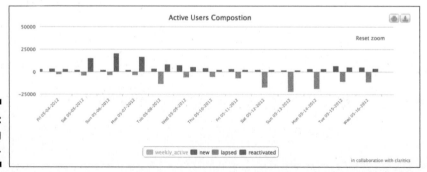

Figure 13-18:
Assessing
churn.

Image courtesy of Badgeville

WARNING!

Even a stable or growing active user base may still be in poor health if lapsing isn't adequately offset by reactivations.

✔ **How long do you keep your users?** To gauge this, look at the progression from week 1 to week *N* retention. You will generally see the number drop sharply from week 1 to week 2 and then gradually level out. Together with return rates, weekly retention metrics give you a good picture of how sustainable your growth is. Ideally, you want good long-term retention numbers together with a solid weekly return rate. This signals that you keep your users long term — and keep them engaged in the process.

✔ **How repeatable are the activities on your site?** To answer this, look for the distribution of the number of times an activity is repeated by the same user over a one-week period (see Figure 13-19). This information will help you determine where to set the threshold for the number of activities of a certain type required to earn a reward. For example, if you want to reward people for sharing ten times per week on Facebook, but the chart shows that virtually no one shares more than five times per week, you'll probably want to lower that bar. (Remember, some goals should be easy, whereas others should be more of a stretch.)

Figure 13-19:
Viewing the activities per distribution can help you determine where to set your reward thresholds.

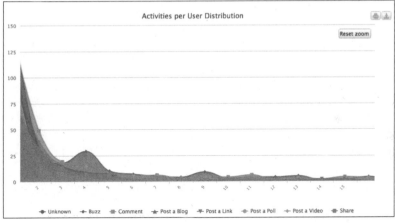

Image courtesy of Badgeville

Healthy, Wealthy, and Wise: Using the Behavior Health Index (BHI)

One more tool for gauging the effectiveness of your gamification program, you can rely on what's called the Behavior Health Index — BHI for short. It offers a simple, concise way to measure the overall performance of your gamified digital property, web site, or mobile application.

The BHI combines the measurements of user base growth, engagement, retention, and conversion into a single metric, giving you an immediate status and performance check. With the BHI, you can tell in an instant how your gamified program is doing as you compare your site's metrics against your own historical baseline. The BHI provides a meaningful starting point from which you can gain valuable insight to tune and optimize your overall experience.

As mentioned, the BHI is built from four separate components:

- **User base growth (people):** Although the overall volume of your user base is important, you also want to explore the percentage of users who are highly engaged, as well as those who have one-and-done experiences every week, month, or year. For customer-facing experiences, this could include understanding the number of active users on your online communities and websites. For an employee-facing scenario, it might be the user base of your CRM or document-management system. Specifically, you want to measure cumulative users (the total number of unique users who have logged on to your site or application to date), active users (the number of people actively using your site or app by day, week, or month), and churn (the number of users who give up on using your site or application).

- **Level and frequency of engagement with the product (engagement):** As you've probably noticed, engagement is a big buzzword, with lots of different meanings. At its most basic level, though, engagement is about getting people to do more stuff, whether it's getting a customer to write a product review or encouraging a sales rep to update a lead. For the purposes of the BHI, you want to gauge engagement by measuring total behaviors (the overall list of behaviors that matter to your user base and the total volume in which they're performed), segmented by type; activities per distribution (which activities your users are performing the most); visit frequency (how often people log in to engage with your site); and time on site/app (how much time of their day, week, month, or year they spend interacting with your products or performing key business processes).

- **User retention (retention):** Ultimately, the goal of your engagement program is to improve the overall stickiness of your site or app. This generates the customer loyalty or employee performance you need to meet your business objectives. On a website, this means getting users to come back frequently to engage with your products or content. For an employee-facing site, that might mean getting people to log in every day to collaborate with each other. When it comes to tracking retention, keep two key metrics in mind: return rate (how often users come back in a given period) and retention rate (how many new users who showed up at your site returned within a set span of time).

- **Customer conversion (conversion).** As customers become more loyal to your products and online communities, or as your employees become more engaged with your various enterprise apps, you'll likely see in increase in key business conversions. On a customer-facing site, this might mean more people purchase your products. On an employee-facing application, this could include an increase in the number of deals closed. Generally, the more you grow the first three components of the BHI (people, engagement, and retention), the better chance you have of improving your conversions. Key metrics pertaining to conversion include anonymous to registered users (the number of people who upgrade from guest to member status), buy clicks and purchases (the number of people who click to put items on their cart and/or make purchases), business process completion (the number of business processes completed), and free to paid users (the number of people who upgrade from free trials to paid subscriptions).

The Behavior Health Index is an average of performance in those four key areas:

BHI = ¼ People + ¼ Engagement + ¼ Retention + ¼ Conversion

Ordinarily, if your organization were to have a perfect BHI score, it would add up to 100. Note, though, that the BHI can also be modular and flexible, weighting one category more than the others. For example, some online communities might be less concerned with conversions if the goal of the community is for users to share content with each other. In that case, the people, retention, and engagement metrics would be weighted more heavily.

At its core, the BHI is a benchmarking tool. The most basic application of BHI is the single score that gives you an immediate and concise piece of information to judge your program's performance. From there, it's easy to dive to greater levels of insight as you compare it against your own historical scores or against other sites and applications in the same vertical as you.

To facilitate graphical interpretation of the scores, you can use two different kinds of visualizations. The first is a simple bar chart for the four metric categories (see Figures 13-20 and 13-21).

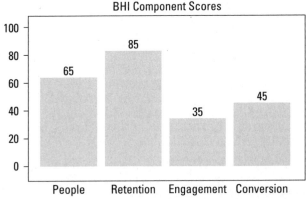

Figure 13-20: This simple bar chart shows the score for each of the four performance scores.

Illustration by Wiley, Composition Services Graphics

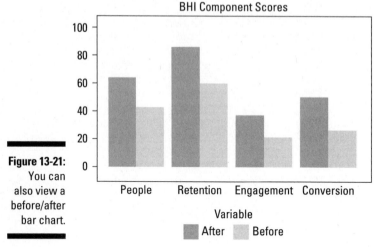

Figure 13-21: You can also view a before/after bar chart.

You could also view the components of the BHI on a radar plot. A *radar plot* consists of a sequence of spokes, or radii, with each representing one of the variables — in this case, People, Retention, Engagement, and Conversion. Here, maximum possible performance is indicated by a diamond covering these four radii. An actual site's data will cover a subset of this diamond's total area, as will the vertical it is matched up against (see Figure 13-22).

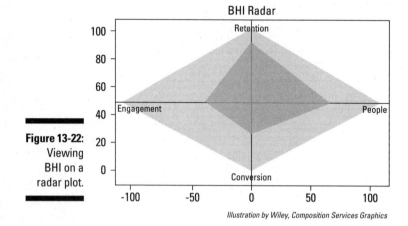

Figure 13-22: Viewing BHI on a radar plot.

Chapter 14

What's Next: The Future of Gamification

. . . .

In This Chapter

▶ Exploring the Pew Report on gamification

▶ Discovering future trends in gamification

. . . .

By now, you have a solid understanding of what gamification is and where it's been. But where's it going? Obviously, we're not psychic. But we're starting to see some evolution in gamification, and from that we can extrapolate where it might wind up. In this chapter, you'll get an idea of what could be just around the bend.

Digging into the Pew Report on Gamification

In May of 2012, the Pew Research Center's Internet & American Life Project, in conjunction with Elon University's Imagining the Internet Center, released a study titled "The Future of Gamification." The study, available online at www.pewinternet.org/Reports/2012/Future-of-Gamification.aspx, cites the results of a survey in which researchers asked more than 1,000 technology stakeholders which of the following two statements they agreed with, and to elaborate on their answer:

> ✔ By 2020, gamification (the use of game mechanics, feedback loops, and rewards to spur interaction and boost engagement, loyalty, fun and/or learning) will not be implemented in most everyday digital activities for most people. While game use and game-like structures will remain an important segment of the communications scene and will have been adopted in new ways, the gamification of other aspects of communications will not really have advanced much beyond being an interesting development implemented occasionally by some segments of the population in some circumstances.

> ✔ By 2020, there will have been significant advances in the adoption and use of gamification. It will be making waves on the communications scene and will have been implemented in many new ways for education, health, work, and other aspects of human connection, and it will play a role in the everyday activities of many of the people who are actively using communications networks in their daily lives.

The result? Forty-two percent of respondents agreed with the first statement, whereas 53 percent agreed with the second. (Note that although respondents were instructed to vote for one scenario over the other, many noted in their explanation that both outcomes were likely to some degree.)

As an aside, the survey surfaced two amusing alterna-words for gamification: *playbor*, a portmanteau for *play* plus *labor*, and *weisure*, an amalgam of *work* and *leisure*.

Obviously, we're with the latter group — the 53 percent. We believe that, as one respondent so aptly put it, "Playing beats working. So if the enjoyment and challenge of playing can be embedded in learning, work, and commerce, then gamification will take off."

And we're not the only ones. Gartner, the famous technology consultancy, predicts that by 2015, 50 percent of corporate innovation will be gamified. And Deloitte, another major consulting firm, included gamification as one of its Top 10 Technology Trends of 2012, noting that "Serious gaming simulations and game mechanics such as leaderboards, achievements, and skill-based learning are becoming embedded in day-to-day business processes, driving adoption, performance, and engagement."

It bears saying that the aforementioned survey was conducted, according to the study's authors, "to help accurately identify current attitudes about the potential future for networked communications and are not meant to imply any type of future forecast." So, like, don't go to Vegas and lay down your life savings on the results. But the very fact that a Pew study has been conducted on the topic of gamification indicates that it's becoming a "thing."

Tracking the Trends in Gamification

You don't need a crystal ball to get some idea of where gamification may be headed. Instead, take a look at some current trends and make an educated guess as to what might come next.

Many see gamification becoming part of a greater business discipline called behavior lifecycle management (BLM). If you want to have an ongoing relationship with your customer or continue to see employees optimize their various technology resources, you need to constantly iterate on the behaviors that matter to them at that particular point in time.

Big data

Over the last few years, the amount of online data available to marketers has exploded. And it's like gold. To say that this data may hold the key to your organization's success is no exaggeration. After all, if you understand your customer data, you essentially know your future. Based on this data, you can segment your users, target them, make recommendations, and more. That is amazingly valuable in this world.

The fact is, whoever has the most data has the most power. The challenge? Doing stuff with that data. Everyone is gathering the gold, but people are just now figuring out how to derive meaning from it and making it work for them.

This trend, often called *big data* (not to be confused with *Big Daddy*, starring Adam Sandler), is the wind in the sails of gamification. Thanks to big data, we can capture, store, and process loads of data; we can then use that data to determine which game mechanics will drive valuable behaviors. Then we can collect yet more information about the effectiveness of those mechanics, upon which we can then act to drive yet more behaviors, and so on, *ad infinitum*. This data is extremely relevant because it's tied directly to behaviors — behaviors that directly affect revenue and those that affect revenue indirectly. It's relevant to an organization's bottom line.

Gamification and the analytics used with gamification change — and will continue to change — big data into big *actionable* data. Without actionable data, you'd simply be gathering all this information but wouldn't have any context for it. All you could do is look for — if you'll excuse the metaphor — Jesus in the tortilla. As in, "I'm scouring all this data; please, God, for the love of all that is holy, let it bring some kind of revelation." With actionable data, you can actually move the needle on the behaviors you want to encourage *without* pleading to a deity, and you will be able to see the impact on your business.

Segmenting Data

Speaking of big data and gamification: In addition to enabling you to gather actionable data, these trends also help you to understand your users better. Specifically, you can view all that data you glean through your gamification program and other information-gathering efforts in user segments, a practice called — you guessed it — *segmentation*. As the smart folks at Wikipedia put it, segmentation is "a marketing strategy that involves dividing a broad target market into subsets of consumers who have common needs and applications for the relevant goods and services."

On the topic of Wikipedia, you could easily make the case that the famous user-generated encyclopedia is a loose example of gamification, with your "score" being the number of edits you make to the site. After all, what better way to motivate millions of people to create and maintain an enormous Web-based encyclopedia — *for free*?

How is segmentation helpful? Simple. Segmentation helps you understand your audience. For example, you might segment the audience by age and gender, location, income . . . whatever criteria you choose. Segmenting your data in this manner makes it *way* easier to spot trends among various groups — not to mention devise gamification programs, marketing campaigns, and rewards specifically for each segment.

The bottom line: As gamification continues to evolve, you'll see more and more ways to segment your user data and act upon it more effectively.

Portable reputation

One of the great things about gamification is that it enables people to build — and share — their reputation on a site. For example, say you're crazy active on a community forum that centers around routers. That is, you're a regular contributor. You frequently answer questions posed by other community members, and your responses are usually upvoted or liked. As a result, you've earned the status of Level 10 Router God.

But then you decide to start visiting a community forum on a different site. Suddenly, you're back to Level 1 Newbie, at least, as far as members of that new forum are concerned. You're merely one of the undifferentiated masses. That's where *portable reputation* comes in. With portable reputation, you would carry your reputation from the first site to the second one — and beyond.

The fact is, people really care about their reputation, rank, expertise, and identity, and they love to be accorded the respect they deserve. With portable reputation, you don't have to start from scratch, building your reputation at each site. Instead, you carry your reputation with you wherever you go. Your reputation could even be visible on job-related sites like LinkedIn or Monster.com, improving your odds in a job search.

Portable reputation is a good thing for companies, too. On the employee side, having access to people's behavior data (as opposed to information they've supplied themselves, which may or may not be accurate) makes it easier to make good hires. And having experts deign to visit your organization's community will reflect well on your offering there, too. The result: more interaction, more collaboration, more efficiency, more sharing of knowledge, and more productivity. But the big opportunity here is on the customer side: getting consumer information in a retail environment.

Social listening

These days, a lot of companies engage in what they call *social listening*. That is, they listen to all the conversations happening across various social media channels — Facebook, Twitter, Linked In, blogs, forums, and so forth — to find out who's talking about them (positively or negatively) and to get a handle on how well their social media efforts are doing in general. The problem? On its own, this information isn't terribly actionable. You're listening to what's going on, but beyond that, there's nothing you can do.

Enter gamification. More and more, gamification will be coupled with social listening. The idea will be to use social listening to listen for the different behaviors customers are performing and then try to find ways to reward them through gamification. The result? More *actionable* information.

The merging of online and offline worlds

EMC, an American company that sells data-storage products and services, hosts a gamified community. Recently, the company went one step farther, merging its online environment with the offline world by gamifying its annual conference, EMC World.

Here are a few examples of steps EMC took to conflate these two worlds:

✔ The online reputation and identity of conference participants were reflected in their offline materials (name badges and so on).

✔ Checking in at real-world locations using mobile devices or by scanning badges garnered the participants virtual rewards.

✔ Certain real-world behaviors were rewarded, such as stopping by specific booths at the tradeshow or attending certain seminars.

Of course, EMC isn't the only organization that's messing around with the merging of online and offline worlds through gamification. Indeed, there's a whole movement that shares these same aims, loosely led by one Seth Priebatsch, CEO of SCVNGR, a Google-backed game company. Priebatsch notes that the last decade was all about social — Facebook, Twitter, and so on. But the next decade, says Priebatsch, is going to be about games. Priebatsch's goal is to add what he calls a *game layer* to the real world — what the folks at TED (the famous nonprofit devoted to spreading great ideas) describe as "a pervasive net of behavior-steering game dynamics."

In a recent presentation at the South by Southwest (SXSW) conference, Priebatsch pitched his vision, noting that "Unlike the social layer, which trafficked in connections, the game layer traffics in influence." More importantly, Priebatsch asserts that the game layer can be about more than just having fun; it could help solve the world's problems — from boring schools to global warming and beyond. The game layer — which, Priebatsch says, could be ten times as large as the social layer — "can move something that's impossible to something that's just difficult."

Priebatsch isn't the only one who's hit on this idea. Another key figure is game designer and author Jane McGonigal. She writes and speaks on the topic of how alternate reality games and massively multiplayer online games can be used to improve quality of life, arguing that in-game behavior and values can translate into solutions to real world problems such as poverty, disease, and hunger.

The subtleization of gamification

In its current incarnation, gamification is rather overt. There are badges. There are leaderboards. It's like, you can't miss it. But over time, we believe gamification will become more subtle. Softer. Less overt. Gamification programs will become so seamless that they'll be almost unnoticeable.

At the same time, we think gamification will be built into everything, the way Like buttons have made social media ubiquitous. Indeed, we think gamification will be so prevalent that its absence — rather than its presence — will seem glaring.

As gamification becomes less overt and explicit, we think people will begin to gamify the system themselves. For example, take Twitter. You may not think of Twitter as a gamified site, but one could make the case that it is — and the number of followers you have is your score (see Figure 14-1). What's interesting about Twitter, though, is that apart from that score, there is no overt gamification. There may not be badges or leaderboards per se. You don't know where you rank in terms of number of followers relative to other Twitter users. Even so, who doesn't look at her own score and self-gamify by setting little goals to increase it? (Be honest.) The beauty of this is it's much more flexible than explicitly gamifying the site.

Figure 14-1:
Clearly, this guy is winning at Twitter.

Image courtesy of Kris Duggan

From game to narrative

In addition to becoming less overt, we think gamification will shift from *funware*, (to borrow a term coined by gamification enthusiast Gabe Zichermann — meaning the use of game mechanics such as points, leaderboards, badges, and such in non-game contexts to encourage specific behaviors by users) — to become a means by which the user is taken on a personal journey. That is, rather than being explicitly fun, gamification will put a narrative around the user's experience. (Indeed, this shift has already begun; it's the whole premise behind reputation mechanics.)

This means, by extension, that game mechanics will not be static. They'll be matched to the user's experience on the site (or, to be fancy and quite serious sounding, the user's *life stage*). That is, you'll have different mechanics for new users, existing users, and power users. You could also match game mechanics to each user's play pattern, or Bartle player type.

You learned about the Bartle player types in Chapter 2. To refresh your memory, Bartle identified four player types: explorers (people who like to dig around), achievers (people who are in it to win it), socializers (people who are more interested in meaningful social interaction), and killers (people who don't just want to win; they want to humiliate their foes in the process). They shouldn't be taken as some kind of science, but as a tool to help you identify various types of users on your site.

Part IV
The Part of Tens

The 5th Wave   By Rich Tennant

"My company's instituting a new gamification plan, so I told my wife playing the new Halo game was vital to my career success."

In this part . . .

We offer our (admittedly unsolicited) opinions on a variety of topics — namely, ten additional reading resources, ten great gamified sites and apps, ten reasons gamification is great in areas involving sales, communities, and so on. Plus an appendix to help you supercharge your sales team.

Chapter 15

Ten Additional Gamification Resources

In This Chapter
▶ Books about games, gamification, and reputation systems
▶ Volumes about human behavior

Can't get enough of this discussion? Neither can we. That's why this chapter lists ten additional books for you to expand your knowledge.

Some of these books relate primarily to gamification and related topics, such as reputation systems; others take on the larger topics of motivation, persuasion, change, habits, and human behavior.

If you're ready to expand your knowledge in these fascinating areas, get reading!

"Building Web Reputation Systems" by Randy Farmer and Bryce Glass

Interested in learning more about reputation systems? Then *Building Web Reputation Systems* (O'Reilly, 2010) is for you. Written by experts who designed Web communities for Yahoo! and other sites, it shows you how to design and develop a reputation system for your own site or application in the vein of the systems found on such sites as Amazon.com, eBay, Slashdot, and Xbox Live.

You'll discover why reputation systems are critical to sites that depend on users for content, how to encourage first-class contributions, how to filter less-than-stellar contributions, and how best to engage and reward contributors.

"Persuasive Technology" by B. J. Fogg

Don't think computers can motivate people? Dr. B.J. Fogg, director of the Persuasive Technology Lab at Stanford University, is here to disabuse you of that notion. (Remember him? We mention him in Chapter 2.)

Fogg's book *Persuasive Technology: Using Computers to Change What We Think and Do* (Morgan Kaufmann, 2002) assembles nine years of research in *captology* (a phrase Fogg coined to describe the domain of research, design, and applications of persuasive computers) to reveal how technology can be — and is — used to change people's attitudes and behavior. If you're a technology designer, marketer, researcher, consumer, or just someone who wants to understand the persuasive power of interactive technology, then this book is for you. Oh, and don't let its publication date fool you — much of what's in Dr. Fogg's book is timeless.

"Reality Is Broken" by Jane McGonical

Fun fact: There are more than 174 million gamers in the United States alone. Indeed, by the time he turns 21, the average American will have logged more than 10,000 hours gaming. Why? According to visionary game designer Jane McGonigal's book *Reality Is Broken: Why Games Make Us Better and How They Can Change the World* (Penguin, 2011), it's because video games frequently fulfill human needs.

Moreover, asserts McGonigal — who draws on psychology, cognitive science, and sociology to support her claims — games can be used to fix what's wrong with the *real* world, from social problems such as depression and obesity to global ones like poverty and client change.

"Total Engagement" by Byron Reeves and J. Leighton Read

Millions of people spend hours every day engaged in online gameplay. In their book *Total Engagement: Using Games and Virtual Worlds to Change the Way People Work and Businesses Compete* (Harvard Business School Press, 2009), Reeves and Read want to show readers how to foster that same level of engagement by bringing game environments to work. Their theory: By implementing elements of games in the workplace, you can solve a host of

If you're looking to persuade others to comply, then this book (published by Harper Business in 2006) — written in a narrative style and featuring scholarly research — is a great place to start.

"The Power of Habit" by Charles Duhigg

Why do habits exist? How important are they to success? How can they be changed? These are the key questions addressed by *New York Times* business reporter Charles Duhigg in *The Power of Habit: Why We Do What We Do in Life and Business* (Random House, 2012).

Using a diverse array of examples — Olympic swimmer Michael Phelps, Starbucks CEO Howard Schultz, civil-rights hero Martin Luther King Jr., Procter & Gamble, Target, Rick Warren's Saddleback Church, NFL locker rooms, and the nation's largest hospitals — Duhigg illustrates how the right habits can mean the difference between failure and success, or even life and death.

"Switch" by Chip Heath and Dan Heath

In *Switch: How to Change Things When Change Is Hard* (Crown Business, 2010), brothers Chip Heath and Dan Heath team up to demonstrate that successful change often follows a pattern and that you can harness that same pattern to make changes in your own life.

The primary obstacle, note the authors — who lean on decades of research in psychology, sociology, and other fields — is a conflict that's hard-wired in our brains between the rational mind (the one that wants the body of a 21-year-old Olympic swimmer) and the emotional mind (the one that really wants a slice of cheesecake and a nap). By uniting these two minds, they say, change can occur. If you want to make change in your life your work, then you'll love this book.

"Thinking, Fast and Slow" by Daniel Kahneman

Thinking, Fast and Slow (Farrar, Straus and Giroux, 2011) — cited by the *New York Times Book Review*, *Globe and Mail*, *The Economist*, and *TheWall Street Journal* as one of the best books of 2011— will transform the way you think about . . . thinking.

problems — such as morale, communication, and business alignment. At the same time, this approach improves skills from data analysis, to teamwork, to recruitment, to leadership, and beyond.

"Gamification by Design" by Gabe Zichermann and Christopher Cunningham

In addition to touching on the gamification basics — core game mechanics, rewards, and so on — this book gets more into the nitty gritty of *how* to implement a gamification program on any type of consumer-facing Web site or mobile app, including meaningful code examples. *Gamification by Design: Implementing Game Mechanics in Web and Mobile Apps* (O'Reilly, 2011) also offers case studies that help *firmalize* (like that word? we made it up) your knowledge.

"Predictably Irrational" by Dan Ariely

Although you may believe you act rationally, the fact is — no offense —you probably don't, at least some of the time. Even so, notes *New York Times* bestselling author Dan Ariely in his book *Predictably Irrational: The Hidden Forces that Shape Our Decisions* (Harper Perennial, 2010), those behaviors aren't random. In his view, they're both systematic and predictable, making us, as he says, "predictably irrational." Presenting a wide range of scientific experiments, findings, and anecdotes, Ariely challenges readers to rethink what makes them — and the people around them — tick.

"Influence: The Psychology of Persuasion" by Robert B. Cialdini

Author Robert Cialdini has worked as a salesperson, fundraiser, and advertiser, among other positions. In other words, he's built a career on getting people to say yes. During that time, he's recognized various compliance techniques, which he organizes into six categories: reciprocation, consistency, social proof, liking, authority, and scarcity.

Kahneman, a recipient of the Nobel Prize in Economic Sciences, explains the two systems of the mind that drive *how* we think. One is fast, intuitive, and emotional. The other is slower, more deliberative, and more logical. He then discusses the extraordinary capabilities of *fast thinking*, as well as the faults and biases, before revealing when we should mistrust our intuitions and instead engage in *slow thinking*. If you're looking for no-nonsense and eye-opening insights into how choices get made — critical information for anyone attempting to drive behaviors — then this book is for you.

"Drive" by Daniel Pink

Okay, we said this chapter contains ten additional resources, but we couldn't bear to leave this one out. Consider it a bonus.

In *Drive: The Surprising Truth About What Motivates Us* (Riverhead, 2011), *New York Times* bestselling author Daniel Pink observes that most people believe that rewards are the key to motivation — the traditional carrot-and-stick model. But according to Pink, what *really* motivates people are three things: autonomy (the need to direct our own lives), mastery (the drive to learn and create new things), and purpose (the need to do better by ourselves and our world). These intrinsic motivators are, he notes, far more powerful than extrinsic ones, such as money or stuff.

This big-idea book offers, well, big ideas on how to make work more fulfilling.

Chapter 16

Ten Great Gamified Sites and Apps

In This Chapter

▶ Discovering great gamified sites

▶ Exploring fun gamified apps

By now, you're probably eager to see some examples of gamification in action. Lucky you!

This chapter lists ten sites and/or apps that feature smart gamification — some overtly, others more subtly.

eBay (www.ebay.com)

eBay has long used a points system to enable users to show their status on the site. And they've demonstrated the importance of reputation as a reward to both buyers and sellers, even issuing badges to those sellers they deem to be the best. As you no doubt have learned, these are key game mechanics.

In the future, look to eBay to gamify more aspects of its site to make it even more engaging.

Foursquare (www.foursquare.com)

Foursquare is a free mobile app (see Figure 16-1) that enables you to "check in" at various places and share your experiences there. As you do, Foursquare rewards you with points and badges. You might even get special deals, such as a discount off your bill at a restaurant or a freebie for bringing your friends.

You can also use Foursquare to get recommendations for what to do next. Check in at a given place enough times, and you may become its "mayor" — which can bring with it its own set of privileges, such as a special parking space.

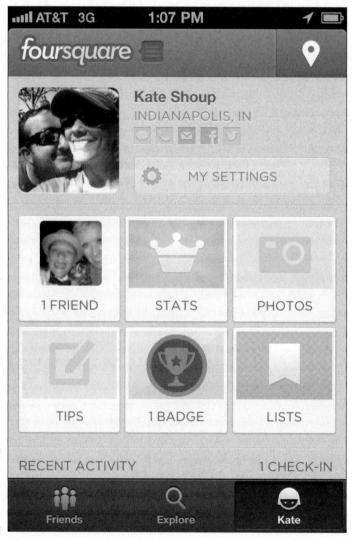

Figure 16-1: Check in with Foursquare.

GetGlue (www.getglue.com)

GetGlue is a little like FourSquare — except that instead of checking in at their favorite restaurants, shops, and such, GetGlue users check in while watching shows, listening to music, reading books, or engaging in other entertainment-related activities.

In return, users get relevant recommendations, exclusive *stickers* (like badges), discounts, and other rewards, such as goodies from their favorite shows or movies.

Mint (www.mint.com)

Mint.com wants to help members get a handle on their finances, and it uses subtle gamification — primarily in the form of progress bars and fun feedback — to make it happen. Members can also post details about their financial goals online to increase their chances that those goals will be met.

This site is a great example of a less-overt form of gamification — there are no badges or prizes, but the game mechanics in place are effective nonetheless.

MuchMusic.com (www.muchmusic.com)

MuchMusic, Canada's MTV-equivalent, gamified its site with its MuchCloser program. Members of MuchCloser get points for doing all the stuff they normally do on the site — watching videos, reading blogs, leaving comments, sharing content, and so forth.

As the points pile up, users unlock rewards and trophies and become eligible for prizes and giveaways. The most active users are flagged as key members of the MuchMusic community.

Nike+ (www.nikeplus.nike.com)

Nike+ is a fitness-oriented service that enables you to log your physical activity using a mobile app or other Nike gear. When you do, you earn NikeFuel, which is a super-cool alterna-word for points.

As you earn more NikeFuel, you unlock awards, trophies, and surprises — not to mention a banging physique. In the mood to brag? Share your accomplishments with your friends and with other Nike+ members.

Recyclebank (www.recyclebank.com)

Recyclebank gives members points for taking "everyday green actions" such as using less water, recycling, making greener purchases, using energy more efficiently, or even walking to work instead of driving. For even more points, members can take online quizzes about ecology and share information from the site with friends on Facebook, Twitter, and mobile applications.

Users can redeem points for goodies such as gifts and flowers, books and magazines, health and beauty items, and music with participating local and national partners.

Samsung (www.samsung.com)

Samsung's social loyalty program, Samsung Nation, makes excellent use of gamification to recognize and empower the company's most passionate fans. When you join Samsung Nation, you can earn points, level up, unlock badges, and gain entry into various contests and promotions by performing such behaviors as watching videos, commenting on articles, reviewing products, participating in user-generated Q&As, and more.

Top users appear on the Samsung Nation leaderboard, and an activity stream keeps users up to date on the site's goings-on.

sneakpeeq (www.sneakpeeq.com)

A retail site, sneakpeeq offers discounted goodies, from gourmet foods, to home products, to accessories, to apparel, and from big labels like Kate Spade and Puma to smaller brands. The twist? The site is gamified to make shopping more fun.

The more you buy, share, *love* (similar to *liking* an item) and *peeq* (viewing an item's price), the more badges and rewards you unlock, and the more incentives and surprises you receive. Leaderboards make the experience more social and competitive, kind of like throwing an elbow at a sample sale.

Xbox Live (www.xbox.com)

First came Shakespeare with his "play within a play." Now there's Xbox, with its "game within a game." That is, Xbox, itself a game platform, uses elements of gamification . . . *within its games.*

Specifically, users can earn achievement points, referred to as *gamerscore*, by performing specific tasks or actions in a game. This gamerscore is separate from the player's score in the game itself and is a way of conveying the player's reputation across the platform, including its social spaces (see Figure 16-2).

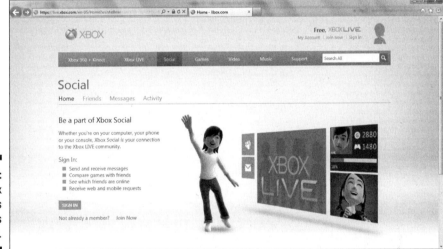

Figure 16-2:
Xbox
Live has
gamified its
games.

Image courtesy of Xbox Live

Appendix

Supercharge Your Sales Team with Gamification

Sales teams are particularly susceptible to the dangers of employee disengagement. Despite extraordinary spending toward sales-based applications, training, and compensation, companies face several critical impediments to success in the areas of onboarding, retention, motivation, tool adoption, collaboration, and quota achievement. Sales tenure is short, turnover is high, and training is forgotten. More than 50 percent of sales managers report that their sales reps do not adopt CRM tools, leading to the failure of half of CRM implementations. This comes with real costs: 10 percent of annual revenue lost and a 7 percent drop in quotas met.

Gamification helps engage sales employees and improve collaboration among teams by allowing sales management to reward the behaviors that drive company goals and provide positive reinforcement during the sales process instead of simply reacting once the results are in and relying on the fear of punishment for underperformance. In reality, sales organizations are already familiar with basic forms of gamification, such as leaderboards and President's Clubs for top performers. Incorporating a modern gamification program allows a deep integration with company CRM sheets with differing rules and mismatched data. Companies can realize increased productivity, faster conversions, a faster sales cycle, and an increase in app adoption. More simply, they realize more value from their CRM investments. Plus, because the gamification is embedded in the CRM, it can promote the minute, exact behaviors within the sales process that are necessary to create consistent success. Employees, for their part, gain recognition for their achievements and get to have a bit more fun while doing the things that help them reach individual and company goals.

The Drastic Cost of a Disengaged Sales Force

Companies are facing an engagement crisis among their ranks. In October, 2011, Gallup reported that 71 percent of employees are either "not engaged" with or "actively disengaged" from their work, meaning they are less likely to be productive. This lack of productivity is not unique to sales organizations, but it is a particular danger to them, as sales productivity translates directly into revenue. Executives and managers must keep sales employees motivated to continue hitting the numbers.

Traditionally, organizations have thrown a lot of money at this problem, with the tendency to buy more sales apps to supplant the ones that "aren't work-ing," with unclear results. Gamification, however, can be a highly effective tool for organizations to engage and motivate their sales employees, and it works by incentivizing people to use existing sales applications more effec-tively instead of replacing the applications with new ones. It also augments the traditional, overwhelmingly output-based and negative-reinforcement heavy sales-management mindset with a framework that helps drive the important behaviors that lead to sales success. Combining game mechanics, reputation mechanics, and social mechanics, gamifying CRM helps organiza-tions re-engage their sales teams for success.

Engagement Makes a Difference

One could ask in the first place whether employee engagement really makes a difference. It does. A Gallup survey reports that customer engagement was positively influenced by an increase in employee engagement. In the underly-ing study, employees at a large financial-services company were divided into groups over a four-month period. In one group, engagement was fostered, while the other acted as a control group. At the end of the period, the test group saw an 83 percent increase in employee engagement, versus a 19 per-cent increase in the control group. More interestingly, though, the test group saw a 28 percent increase in customer engagement, versus an increase of only 5 percent in the control group. More engaged employees lead to more engaged customers.

Achieving that employee engagement isn't easy, though. Sales organizations face the following engagement challenges:

✔ **Onboarding:** 84 percent of sales training is forgotten in a mere 90 days, even though organizations spent another $5 billion on training and per-formance improvement in 2011.

- **Retention:** The average inside sales organization faces 33 percent turn-over every year.

- **Motivation:** Most sales apps don't give salespeople a way to measure their progress toward a goal, which makes mid-stream adjustments very difficult. They have to wait until they've either reached or failed to reach their goal.

- **Tool adoption:** Half of CRM implementations fail because 50 percent of employees never adopt the new tools that have been provided.

- **Collaboration:** Sales employees have little incentive to input and share the data that CRM installations need to be effective.

- **Quota achievement:** Organizations have seen a 7 percent drop in quotas met.

You Don't Need Another App for That

Sales managers and executives have responded to these challenges in large part by spending money — lots of money — especially on sales apps. In 2011, organizations invested more than $5 billion on sales-based applications, usu-ally with the goal of automating the sales process to improve efficiency. They spent an additional $5 billion on training and performance improvement. To sales compensation (including incentives such as President's Clubs), they devoted a staggering $512 billion — a sum equivalent to 3.5 percent of the United States gross domestic product. This employee disengagement costs companies up to 10 percent in annual revenue. Still, traditional sales thinking remains prevalent in organizations. Indeed, 77 percent of survey respondents reported that their company incentivized salespeople through bonuses, and 20 percent said their company used punishment as a performance incentive. This, even though the measurable results have been unclear at best.

Gamification Embodies the Collaborative Nature of Sales 2.0

Rising to counter these challenges is a change in the way sales teams work, a trend that has the potential to mitigate the problems described above. It's the Sales 2.0 framework, sales expert and Reality Works Group CEO Anneke Seley's term for "the measurably more efficient and effective way of selling for both the buyer and the seller enabled through technology" that began transforming the sales world about three years ago. Through this shift, sales-people have moved from being individual contributors with defined territories of which they have sole ownership to being part of sales teams where emphasis is placed on information sharing and collaboration, both internally and with buyers.

Technologies such as the Force.com platform have enabled this collaborative transition, but they are only as valuable as the data they contain. As Seley herself has said, gamification fits very comfortably within the Sales 2.0 realm. Through thoughtfully implemented game mechanics, businesses can successfully encourage their salespeople to populate the data sales teams (and app installations like Sales force) required to offer value in the modern, collaborative sales environment. Furthermore, because of the social and reputation mechanics built into certain gaming platforms, such as Badgeville's Behavior Platform, you can promote accountability for doing so through integration with social apps like Chatter that publicize users' achievements and rewards.

People Work for More Than Just Money

Why does gamification work? The answer is based on psychology: specifically, the factors that motivate people to act in a certain way. People respond to extrinsic motivations that come from outside themselves. Indeed, gamification makes it easy to provide virtual rewards to people, whether it's by earning a badge for completing certain actions or by awarding privileges to people who've reached a certain status level. When applied correctly, this system of virtual incentives supplements your financial incentives nicely, creating a holistic strategy for driving behavior.

But even more so than by external motivations, people are also propelled by intrinsic motivations, like the opportunity to build a story of personal growth, of challenges overcome, and goals achieved. Equally as important, people like to share their reputation with others. Not only do they want to be able to hit a benchmark to prove that they close deals quickly, for example, but they also want to become known inside the company as a quick closer. That's why some gamification platforms incorporate social and reputation mechanics along with game mechanics.

An additional benefit of social mechanics, beyond providing additional incentive for people to perform behaviors that will lead to rewards, is that it also incentivizes colleagues to do the same. Publishing a salesperson's achievement to a social activity stream, for example, allows her manager to publicly praise that salesperson. And when other salespeople see the boss praising a colleague, they're going to follow in her footsteps so they, too, can be praised. Social mechanics amplify the effect of positive reinforcement throughout the team.

It's about motivation, not games

The very term "gamification" can make it sound as though business is being turned into a game. Because of this, it can engender strong reactions. Effective gamification, however, isn't about games, nor is it about badges or points. It's about taking the interplay of goals, challenges, rewards, and status that makes games so universally popular and fun and applying it to business processes. If we can lead salespeople to accelerate their average sales cycle or close an above-average-revenue deal and make it more fun for them in the process, isn't that a good thing?

Proactive, Positive Reinforcement Builds a Culture of Success

We're not suggesting that you abandon the practice of rewarding success and punishing failure. But by themselves, bonuses and penalties clearly are not enough to turn the tide. Why? Because they're reactive strategies that take place after the results have already come in. If a commercial airliner were headed in the wrong direction, would air traffic control do nothing, wait until the plane landed at the wrong airport, and then punish the pilot? No. They would work with the pilot to make course corrections mid-flight to help the plane land in the right place. Gamification takes the same proactive approach toward improving sales output.

Traditionally, sales is incredibly output-based: Someone either hits the number or he doesn't. Gamification introduces a continual feedback loop into sales management and allows companies to focus on the inputs that lead to success instead of simply waiting for successful outcomes. You know what metrics matter for your sales team and what steps your salespeople must take to hit them. You can build a gamification program around these specific behaviors.

You create a system of virtual rewards to show your team the right things to do. This does more than simply reward people once they achieve success; by providing positive incentives along the way, you teach people the right things to do in order to achieve that success. This helps build a culture in which people are continually aware of whether they are doing the right things to achieve success, and one in which success happens repeatedly as a result of process instead of luck. Salespeople are continually aware of their progress against this process and can adjust as necessary to help reduce and avoid failure. (Not coincidentally, reputation mechanics also allow your top performers to model successful behaviors for your medium- and lower-tier performers.)

Writing a Consistent Story of Success

By introducing this constant feedback loop and allowing salespeople to see the progress they're making in terms of behaviors instead of end results, gamification also lets salespeople build a persistent story of success. That is to say that more than just giving someone one-time recognition for being Salesperson of the Month, for example, it lets that person say "I have closed thirty $10K+ deals this year" and to continually work to increase that number. As discussed, this lets a salesperson build a story of personal growth and success, which is a prime intrinsic motivator. This also allows sales managers to recognize their salespeople for the achievement of more goals — ones that take more time and dedication to achieve — than simply monthly or quarterly awards.

Gamification Provides Real Benefits

Of course, the fact that gamification makes critical sales processes fun and also motivates salespeople wouldn't mean anything if it didn't also make a difference for business. It does:

- Gamification increases overall sales productivity.
- Gamification speeds up conversion of leads to opportunities.
- Gamification speeds up the sales cycle.
- Gamification increases utilization and adoption of the CRM application.

Designing Gamification Programs for Success: Some Tips

The last thing your organization wants is a gamification program that feels "gimmicky" or doesn't focus on necessary business procedures. The best way to avoid these mistakes is to use game mechanics to reward positive behaviors that a sales team is already doing. Knowing which actions map to company or team goals will allow you to reward your team for the right things. Some promising options include:

- ✔ Increasing the number of daily conversations or meetings scheduled
- ✔ Increasing the value or number of qualified opportunities added to the pipe
- ✔ Converting and delivering qualified leads faster than usual
- ✔ Updating an opportunity's probability
- ✔ Closing an opportunity faster than usual
- ✔ Shortening the sales cycle
- ✔ Increasing average deal size
- ✔ Increasing sales or renewals of existing customers
- ✔ Increasing sales of a new product

Most people already use dashboards to track KPIs; this can be a good starting point from which to select your mechanics. Or you may want to test your program on a few sales reps instead of the entire team, to see what the results look like. Regardless, the key is not to invent mechanics and behaviors just for the program. You want to provide positive, real-time feedback and recognition for doing the right things that your team members already know how to do. That way, the program doesn't feel like a gimmick. Instead, it drives people to do the things they need to do to create success for themselves and the company.

Drive Behavior Across Sales, CRM, and Your Larger Business

Building out a gamification program across Sales Cloud is just a first step. With Badgeville for Salesforce, for example, you can also gamify Service Cloud and Force.com apps, and a user's status and reputation follows her across all of them. Why is this a good idea? Because your users aren't sandboxed in a single touchpoint.

When your salespeople move from one sales tool to another or from one platform to another, you don't want them to have to build their reputation from scratch. Part of what makes reputation mechanics so powerful is their portability. Because the gamification program, like Badgeville's Behavior Platform, isn't tied to a single app but sits on a separate layer, a user's reputation can follow him to any ecosystem. Therefore, a company can expand its gamification program beyond sales into CRM, and their users will enjoy the benefits of their reputation inside CRM systems too — and they'll also be incentivized to continue performing beneficial behaviors there to maintain and further that reputation. Gamification's flexibility allows you to extend this capability even further should you want to gamify support, customer communities, marketing, or product. Some gamification providers' platforms, including Badgeville's Behavior Platform, extend to Yammer, Jive, and SharePoint, to name a few.

Conclusion

Gamification allows companies to transcend the traditional, limited, output-based management techniques of the past by focusing on rewarding the inputs that lead to success. It re-engages employees to achieve results for the company based on the behaviors that you decide are necessary. It reduces complexity by integrating with your sales and CRM systems instead of sitting outside of them, like traditional leaderboards or President's Clubs, so data is always up to date. And because it integrates with your existing software and SaaS investments, it allows you to more fully realize value from those investments by encouraging their use, instead of leaving you to continually invest in new solutions to supplant those that go unutilized. Gamification helps you create a repeatable culture of success within your sales organization.

Index

• C •

• *E* •

• *F* •

• S •

Notes

Notes

Notes

Notes

Notes

Notes

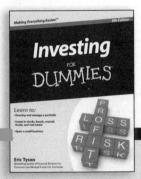
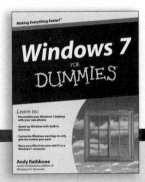
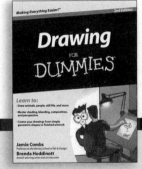

Math & Science

Algebra I For Dummies,
2nd Edition
978-0-470-55964-2

Biology For Dummies,
2nd Edition
978-0-470-59875-7

Chemistry For Dummies,
2nd Edition
978-1-1180-0730-3

Geometry For Dummies,
2nd Edition
978-0-470-08946-0

Pre-Algebra Essentials
For Dummies
978-0-470-61838-7

Microsoft Office

Excel 2010 For Dummies
978-0-470-48953-6

Office 2010 All-in-One
For Dummies
978-0-470-49748-7

Office 2011 for Mac
For Dummies
978-0-470-87869-9

Word 2010
For Dummies
978-0-470-48772-3

Music

Guitar For Dummies,
2nd Edition
978-0-7645-9904-0

Clarinet For Dummies
978-0-470-58477-4

iPod & iTunes
For Dummies,
9th Edition
978-1-118-13060-5

Pets

Cats For Dummies,
2nd Edition
978-0-7645-5275-5

Dogs All-in One
For Dummies
978-0470-52978-2

Saltwater Aquariums
For Dummies
978-0-470-06805-2

Religion & Inspiration

The Bible For Dummies
978-0-7645-5296-0

Catholicism For Dummies,
2nd Edition
978-1-118-07778-8

Spirituality For Dummies,
2nd Edition
978-0-470-19142-2

Self-Help & Relationships

Happiness For Dummies
978-0-470-28171-0

Overcoming Anxiety
For Dummies,
2nd Edition
978-0-470-57441-6

Seniors

Crosswords For Seniors
For Dummies
978-0-470-49157-7

iPad 2 For Seniors
For Dummies, 3rd Edition
978-1-118-17678-8

Laptops & Tablets
For Seniors For Dummies,
2nd Edition
978-1-118-09596-6

Smartphones & Tablets

BlackBerry For Dummies,
5th Edition
978-1-118-10035-6

Droid X2 For Dummies
978-1-118-14864-8

HTC ThunderBolt
For Dummies
978-1-118-07601-9

MOTOROLA XOOM
For Dummies
978-1-118-08835-7

Sports

Basketball For Dummies,
3rd Edition
978-1-118-07374-2

Football For Dummies,
2nd Edition
978-1-118-01261-1

Golf For Dummies,
4th Edition
978-0-470-88279-5

Test Prep

ACT For Dummies,
5th Edition
978-1-118-01259-8

ASVAB For Dummies,
3rd Edition
978-0-470-63760-9

The GRE Test For
Dummies, 7th Edition
978-0-470-00919-2

Police Officer Exam
For Dummies
978-0-470-88724-0

Series 7 Exam
For Dummies
978-0-470-09932-2

Web Development

HTML, CSS, & XHTML
For Dummies, 7th Edition
978-0-470-91659-9

Drupal For Dummies,
2nd Edition
978-1-118-08348-2

Windows 7

Windows 7
For Dummies
978-0-470-49743-2

Windows 7
For Dummies,
Book + DVD Bundle
978-0-470-52398-8

Windows 7 All-in-One
For Dummies
978-0-470-48763-1